GODS AND WORSHIPPERS

GODS AND WORSHIPPERS

IN THE VIKING AND GERMANIC WORLD

THOR EWING

The History Press

for my father

First published 2008

The History Press
The Mill, Brimscombe Port,
Stroud, Gloucestershire, GL5 2QG
www.thehistorypress.co.uk

Reprinted 2010

British Library Cataloguing in Publication Data.
A catalogue record for this book is available from the British Library.

ISBN 978 0 7524 3590 9

Typesetting and origination by
The History Press

CONTENTS

Acknowledgements		6
Introduction		9
Part 1: Rites of the Gods		
Chapter 1	Sacrifice	15
Chapter 2	Invocation	29
Chapter 3	Gods, groves and idols	44
Chapter 4	Temples, priests and festivals	61
Part 2: Another Society		
Chapter 5	Seeresses and seers	83
Chapter 6	Valkyries and norns	98
Chapter 7	Another society	110
Epilogue Rites of the Dead		127
Bibliography		147
Index		156

ACKNOWLEDGEMENTS

I think I have to begin by admitting that I have kept close counsel about some ideas expressed in this book. Without the scope of a book in which to develop the arguments fully, many of these ideas might have sounded somewhat eccentric. Due to this, the list of helpful souls is rather shorter than it might have been.

Nonetheless, whenever I needed help it was always offered and I have to thank Christopher Abram, Gunnar Andersson, Morten Axboe, Tine Bierring, Stefan Brink, Ulla Eriksen, Frog, Åsa Henningsson, Sonja Marzinzik, James Montgomery and Andrew Reynolds for information, help and advice. I have enjoyed help through email discussion groups from Diana Briscoe, Bryan Carella, Anthony Clarke, Sally-Jayne Gilpin, Antoni Grabowski, Kjell Hellesoe, Jonathan Herold, Peter Tunstall, Herwig Weigl, John P. Sexton, Karl Steel and Valerie Wilhite. Useful contributions have also been made by friends outside the field including Arne Andersen, Lukas Thor Dziubalski, Georg Hansen, Torstein Hatlevik, Tone Holte and Brian Holton.

I'd like to thank the many people who have at various times supported and encouraged me with the project. These are too numerous to mention every one individually, but they include Ash Duncan, Alison Finlay, Frog, Richard North, Harriet Tarlo and my undergraduate tutor, John McKinnell, to whom I owe an enormous debt. There are also very many people who have sent me encouraging messages on MySpace and Facebook.

My own perspective is inevitably indebted to the work of generations of scholars. It is not possible to acknowledge such a general debt in all its details, but I am very conscious of the profound influence of many previous scholars, both living and dead. Where I owe a significant specific debt to a more recent scholar, I hope I have always noted this sufficiently, and if any such debts have been overlooked, it is through error rather than intent. More general debts for which I owe acknowledgement include H.R. Ellis Davidson, E.O.G. Turville-Petre and of course Jacob Grimm; everyone working in this field today has at some time been influenced by their ideas and is indebted to their scholarship.

The text was read in its early drafts by Chris Elmes and my wife Annie; without their useful comments and puzzled looks, I am quite sure it would be a lot harder to follow. They also pointed the way towards some interesting additions to the whole. The final text was read by my brother Wolf, who raised more pertinent points of which I have tried to take account. The publishers at Tempus have stood by the project for some years now, and I'd like to thank them all, in particular Peter Kemmis Betty, Tom Vivian, Abigail Green and Wendy Logue for their patience and support.

I'd also like to thank my family: My mother, for her continuing support; my brothers, who have provided stimulating conversation on the subjects of religion and mythology since my early teens; my wife, who not only supported me through the long process of writing the book, but read the drafts and made many useful suggestions, and my children, who have sometimes seen rather less of me than I or they would have wished. Lastly, my father, whose interest in religion and in Anglo-Saxon and Old Norse literature was a profound influence and an inspiration to me, and whose appreciation of my work I valued greatly.

1 This map, which includes information from different historical eras, gives some indication of the fullest extent of the Germanic world. At the end of the Roman period, Germanic peoples emigrated over thousands of miles. However, in some places their cultural influence was weak and evidence from these areas can reflect other cultural traditions

INTRODUCTION

The names of the Germanic gods are spoken every day. Although Saturday takes its name from the Roman Saturn, and Sunday and Monday honour the sun and moon, Tuesday, Wednesday, Thursday and Friday preserve the names of the gods of the Germanic world.

Whilst today most people think of the gods behind these names as Viking gods, they were also the gods of the Anglo-Saxons, of the Franks and Frisians, Ostrogoths and Visigoths, Alamanni and Langobards, and of all the peoples descended from the tribal grouping known to the Romans as Germania, and their story stretches back into prehistory. In this book, I want to look at the religions of all these peoples, and the other myriad tribes of the Germanic diaspora, from their earliest description by Roman writers until the conversion of Scandinavia to Christianity more than 1000 years later (*1*).

I don't mean to argue that the entire Germanic and Scandinavian peoples practised a single universal religion. Clearly, the religion of Roman Germania cannot have been identical with the religion of Viking Scandinavia. Indeed it is in the nature of pre-Christian religion that no definition can be narrow enough to include only a single unified expression of the religion. It is no longer sensible to consider even the religion of Viking Scandinavia as a homogenous whole. Place name studies and other disciplines have revealed important variations between local religious identities.

Any attempt to understand pre-Christian religion presupposes a degree of coherence and consistency which is not necessarily inherent in the complex mosaic of overlapping worldviews we are attempting to describe. This religion was not prescriptive, had no tenets, no creed, no overarching organisation. To understand the nature of pre-Christian religion, we should think instead in terms of individual worshippers, family traditions and regional cults within a broadly consistent framework. It is better, then, to see pre-Christian religion as a system of interlocking and closely interrelated religious worldviews and practices rather than as one indivisible religion.

Over the thousand or more years and the many thousands of square miles which are included in this book, there will have been many variations in the nature of the religion, but what is more remarkable is the number of correspondences which can be identified. To some extent, this continuity is not peculiar to the Germanic and Scandinavian religions, but extends to other religions which we might label with a different cultural or ethnic identity. However, for the purposes of this book, I have limited my field to religious traditions which seem to be firmly rooted among peoples of Germanic origin. These cultures and religions are demonstrably related, and very often they can illuminate each other in important ways.

The main body of this book divides into two parts. Part I looks at the institutions of worship in society as a whole, while Part II identifies a specialist class of religious seers and considers their place relative to mainstream society. An epilogue examines customs relating to death and burial.

There is admittedly a heavy bias towards Scandinavian religion of the Viking Age, which is largely unavoidable. In most areas of research, the evidence from Scandinavia is significantly better than that from England or from continental Europe. Nonetheless, many of the traditions which we can identify in Scandinavia can be recognised in brief glimpses of religious practice from other parts of the Germanic world. In such cases, whilst it would be wrong to pretend that these religious practices were necessarily identical, it would be equally ridiculous to deny that they might well have been very much alike.

Written evidence comes in various forms. There are descriptions by contemporary observers, most often by Romans or Arabs, sometimes by Christian Europeans too; there are accounts by later historians, where mythology is often mixed up with genuine history; there are Christian law codes, penitentials and decrees forbidding pagan practices, and there are Icelandic 'sagas', a word which covers a wide range of literature, from serious attempts at historical accounts (allowing for a certain degree of artistic license) through legendary histories to deliberate fictions. The sagas date mainly from the thirteenth and fourteenth centuries, but they often appear to preserve valuable information about pre-Christian times, which can sometimes be verified by a comparison with independent sources. All these written sources might include, perhaps inevitably include, a degree of colour or bias which might distort the picture they present. However, carefully handled and used in conjunction with other sources, they often reveal rather more than is immediately apparent. Unless otherwise stated, all translations are my own.

A special place is given to poetry, since many surviving poems were originally composed within a pre-Christian context, though often they are difficult to date with any degree of certainty. Early poems were usually passed on for hundreds of years by word of mouth before being written down, and over this time changes might have occurred. However, these poems remain an important source as, beyond a few brief inscriptions, they are as close as we can come to the authentic voice of the pre-Christian world.

As well as the written evidence we have archaeological evidence, which has the virtue of being (usually, at least) an unbiased witness to real events. Unfortunately however, it is often impossible to interpret archaeology without reference to the more fickle historical sources.

A third area of evidence, which I have drawn on from time to time, is found in traditional customs from modern times. It is important to stress that not all traditional customs necessarily reflect pre-Christian religious practices. Nonetheless, there is sometimes a clear trail of evidence linking modern customs with earlier times; some customs are similar to known pre-Christian practices and some were denounced as pagan by early Christian reformers.

Unlike the written traditions of the Germanic world as a whole, through the literature of medieval Iceland, Scandinavian tradition has left us what Johannes Brøndsted called 'a splendid and highly-coloured picture of the old religion ...'. The picture Brøndsted had in mind was in fact largely a picture of Scandinavian mythology, and when we read these myths it is easy to fall under their spell and mistake them for the real essence of the religion. However, the myths were only ever a part of the whole religion. The religious life of Viking Scandinavia also included rituals, prayers, holy sites, priests and seers. Beyond these things, as an expression of a particular outlook or worldview, it was a part of the lived reality of the entire population.

It has often been remarked that the Icelanders have traditionally looked back on their conversion to Christianity not as a 'change of faith' but as a 'change of practice'. Yet surprisingly little attention has been paid to the minutiae of pre-Christian religious practice. This is despite the fact that, without any coherent religious authority or any consistent attempt to define the religion in philosophical terms, it is only in its practice that we can begin to define what pre-Christian religion actually was, or see how the pre-Christian world really worked.

So this book is not a retelling of the myths, nor a search for Indo-European roots or circumpolar analogues. It is not an exhaustive exploration of archaeology, of Latin, Arab or vernacular literatures, or of historical or traditional lore. Neither is it an attempt to define the boundaries of Germanic pre-Christian religion, or to trace the influences and exchanges between various ethnically-defined religions. Although it does synthesise evidence from all these sources, that is not its primary purpose. Rather it is, or is intended as, a vivid sketch of the overall nature and main features of Germanic religion. It looks at religion as it was practised, as it was manifested in society, as what Mauss called a 'total cultural phenomenon', not as a mythology or as a collection of rituals, but as a functional aspect of pre-Christian society and as a forum for that society's relationship with the divine. By addressing questions which have remained not only unanswered, but also unasked, I hope to provide a fresh perspective on all aspects of the pre-Christian world.

The picture of pre-Christian Germanic religion which emerges when one looks at overall patterns and practices rather than at specific gods and myths is recognisably equivalent to that described by Martin of Braga in sixth-century Spain, and also to that which has been described in studies of religion in the early Celtic world. Similarities can also be seen with Hinduism, in historical and contemporary forms, and with other traditional religions of the world.

There are no big explanations in Germanic religion, rather it takes the world as we find it and works with it, recognising it as a complex pattern of powers which are respected, honoured, propitiated or even cajoled. It is in this relationship between powers and people that the religion exists, and though it takes many forms it is fundamentally one of respect, honour and worship – a relationship between gods and worshippers.

PART 1

RITES OF THE GODS

CHAPTER 1
SACRIFICE

BLOOD OFFERING

> The sacrifice is like this: Of all living beings that are male, nine head are offered; by whose blood it is the custom to appease the gods. Their bodies, however, are hung in a grove which is beside the temple. This grove is so sacred to the heathen that the individual trees in it are believed to be holy because of the death or putrefaction of the sacrificial victims. There, even dogs and horses dangle beside people, their bodies hanging jumbled together …
>
> *Gesta Hammaburgensis ecclesiae pontificum*, Bk 4 ch.27

Blood sacrifice was the most powerful offering known to pre-Christian religion. It combined the gift of blood and bones with the offering of life itself. Life, which exists beyond the purely physical, already partakes of the divine. Unlike other offerings which remain in this world even after they have been sacrificed, life is utterly beyond restoration. When life is offered in our world, it is freed to join the gods in theirs.

The sacrifice described above by Adam of Bremen took place every nine years at the pre-Christian royal sanctuary at Uppsala in Sweden. Another eleventh-century account, Thietmar of Merseburg's *Chronicon*, describes a remarkably similar sacrifice at Lejre in Denmark, which also took place every nine years:

> There is the one place in those parts, the chief in the kingdom, called Lejre, in the district known as Zealand, where every nine years, in the month of January (after the time when we celebrate the Lord's Epiphany), everyone gathers, and there they make sacrifice to their gods of ninety nine persons and as many horses, with dogs and cocks (offered in place of hawks) …
>
> *Chronicon*, Bk 1 ch.17

2 Detail of a picture stone from Lärbro Stora Hammars, Gotland, showing images of sacrifice. On the left, a man hangs from a tree, and on the right, another man seems to hold a smaller figure in some kind of structure. The triple triangle or *valknut* is a symbol of the god Odin

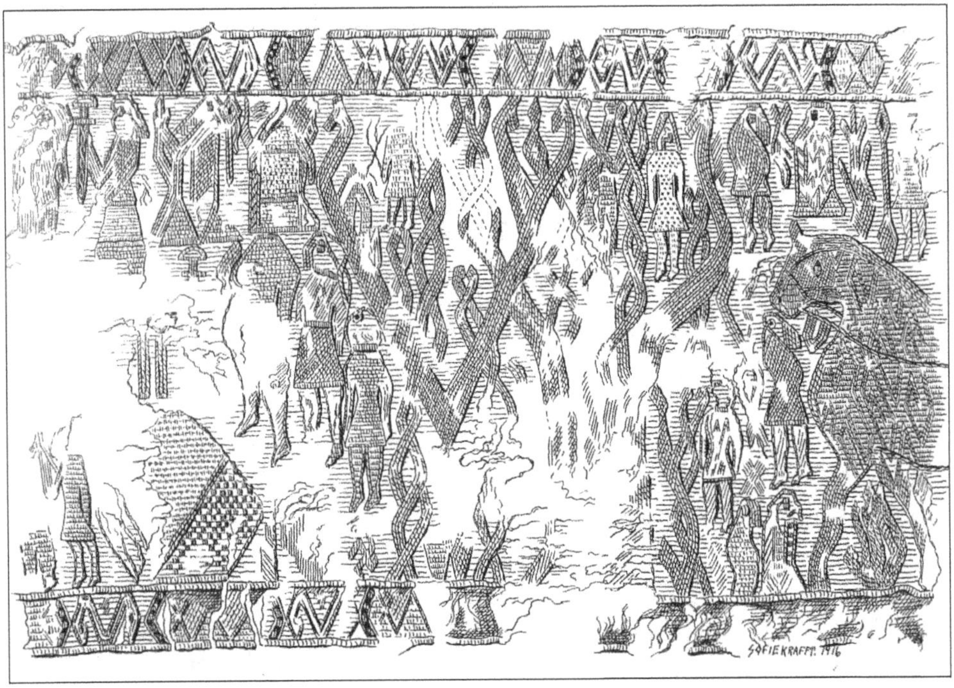

3 A section from the Oseberg Tapestry showing victims hanging in a tree. *Drawing Sofie Krafft*

By the time they were recorded in the eleventh century by Thietmar and Adam, these regular sacrificial rites had been performed by the Germanic peoples for at least a thousand years. The Roman writer Tacitus described the rite as it was practised in his day by the tribes of the Semnones:

> At a set time, in a grove hallowed by the auguries of the fathers and by ancient awe, deputations gather from all peoples of the same blood, and the public sacrifice of a man is the terrible beginning of their barbaric ritual.
>
> *Germania* ch.39

Those bodies of the victims at Uppsala, left to rot in the trees or be eaten as carrion, will have left no trace in the archaeological record. However, at Sutton Hoo in England, a group of 23 burials might represent the bodies of sacrificial victims still clustered around the remains of a sacred tree. At least some of these bodies show evidence of hanging, two are headless and two have had their ankles or wrists tied together. One of the bodies had a collar of organic material around its neck, which was probably the remains of a noose; another grave contained only one long leg bone, suggesting the victim might have hung for some time before burial. The remains of the tree where they met their death were seen by archaeologists as dark marks in the earth, a 'root shadow', indicating that the tree once stood in the centre among the graves.

Like Uppsala, Lejre, and the holy grove of Semnones, Sutton Hoo seems to have been a royal centre and these hanged bodies lie close to the burial mounds of kings. The Sutton Hoo burials might represent the disposal of the bodies of still-hanging victims at the time of the conversion to Christianity.

In Viking times, the ritual of death by hanging seems to have been particularly associated with Odin (2). He himself is hanged on the world tree Yggdrasil in the poem *Hávamál* (st.137-8), and in *Gautreks saga*, King Vikar is hanged with the words, 'Now I give you to Odin' (ch.7). Both Odin and Vikar are also stabbed with a spear as they hang. Nineteenth-century scholars tended to see Odin's self sacrifice as derivative of the death of Christian story, but this is no longer credible. In the poem *Hávamál*, Odin describes his own self sacrifice on the sacred tree Yggdrasil:

> I know that I hung on the windy beam
> for nights of nine,
> gored by the spear and given to Odin,
> myself to myself,
> upon that beam which no one knows
> where the roots of it run.
>
> *Hávamál*, st.138

In sacrifice, the victim in some sense became the god that he was offered to, and it was Odin himself who was killed again. However, in Viking-age Scandinavia death by hanging seems to have been so much the standard form of sacrifice that

4 Detail of a picture stone from Garde Bote, Gotland, which seems to show seven sacrificial maidens

it is possible it was used to offer victims to other gods. Thus, for instance, the hanging bodies at Uppsala might have been dedicated to Frey rather than Odin. Indeed, the medieval Danish historian Saxo says that the Uppsala festival was called 'Frey's Sacrifice' (*Frøblod*) and that human victims were offered to Frey. The Roman historian Tacitus believed that human sacrifice was performed only in honour of Mercury; Roman writers often use the names of their own gods for the gods of other nations, and Mercury is regularly used as an equivalent for Odin or Wodan. Although the historian Jordanes says that victims were dedicated to Mars by hanging (*Getica* Bk 4), Wodan is probably meant here too, as there was no absolute system for translating Roman gods into Germanic gods.

Further evidence of human sacrifice has come from the bogs of Northern Europe, where bodies can be preserved for thousands of years in the peat. Of course, not all bodies from the bogs can be interpreted as victims of sacrifice. Some might have been murdered, and in some cases they might have been accidental deaths, but many examples seem to show evidence of ritual killing, and parallels between examples from different eras and areas suggest that these killings were a cultural phenomenon rather than the work of individuals.

A great number of ancient bog bodies met a violent death, having been strangled, stabbed, hanged, beheaded or drowned. Many were found with nooses or other loops around their necks. Among these, the most famous must be Tollund Man from Denmark (*5*). He was probably about 30 years old when he died, strangled by a leather belt. He was found naked except for his leather hat and belt, but had been laid out with care and his eyes had been closed. Less than a hundred yards away lay the body of Elling woman, whose neck was clearly marked by the leather noose which killed her. At Yde in the Netherlands, a 16-year-old girl had a woollen noose around her neck and at Borremose in Denmark a man had been strangled with a twisted noose.

However, the bodies from the bogs sometimes appear to have been victims of other rites. At Dätgen in northern Germany, a man had been stabbed through the heart, beheaded and flayed, before his body was pegged down with stakes – his head was found some yards away. At Kayhausen in Saxony, a 14-year-old boy had been stabbed in the neck before he was bound hand, foot and neck and then presumably left to drown. From Weerdinge in the Netherlands come two male bodies, one with its bowels falling out of its open belly; reading omens from the entrails of sacrificial victims is mentioned in Willibald's *Vita Bonifatii* ch.6.

The Germanic peoples worshipped a pantheon of several gods, and distinctive sacrificial rites sometimes seem to have been used for individual gods. Although Tacitus suggests that human sacrifice was only offered to Mercury, and indeed the great bulk of later evidence for human sacrifice relates to this god whether as Wotan, Woden or Odin, there is a significant number of sources describing human sacrifice to other gods.

The ninth-century *Berne Scholia* describes how people were burnt in a wooden tub in honour of Taranis, the thunder god. The medieval Icelandic *Eyrbyggja saga* and the Norman historian Dudo of St Quentin both speak of human sacrifices in honour of the Scandinavian thunder god Thor, and in both cases the victim is crushed to death. Both Dudo's account of sacrifice to Thor at the launch of a ship and the *Berne Scholia*'s sacrifice by burning are recalled in the myth of the dwarf Lit, whom Thor kicks into the fire at the launch of Balder's funeral ship. The *Indiculus Superstitionum et Paganiarum*, an eighth-century document which briefly lists 30 signs of paganism, refers to 'spring wells of sacrifice', while Adam of Bremen's account of sacrifices at Uppsala, quoted at the start of this chapter, is expanded by a scholiast, who adds that 'There is also a spring there where the sacrifices of the pagans are habitually performed, and the person is plunged in alive, and if he does not emerge, he is considered the pledge of the people' (ch.26 *schol.*134). Likewise, in *Kjalnesinga saga*, we read that 'men that they were going to sacrifice were thrown down into a fen which was just outside the doors; they called it the 'Sacrifice Pool' (*Blót-keldu*)' (ch.2).

Two forms of sacrifice are attributed to fifth-century Saxon pirates by Sidonius, who notes that they sacrifice one in ten of their prisoners, either to the sea or by 'crucifixion', suggesting that two separate gods were propitiated (Letter to Namatius, *Epistolae* Bk 8). A variety of modes of sacrifice are recorded in *Vatzdæla saga*, and each of these might have honoured a different god:

5 The body of Tollund Man from Bjældskovdal, Jylland, Denmark. After his death by strangulation, his body was laid out with care and his eyes closed. The leather noose which killed him is still about his neck. *Courtesy of Silkeborg Museum*

> If men be put on a skerry, the man is called a 'skerry corpse'; if a man is put in a grave, he is called a 'grave corpse'; if a man is taken onto the fell or into a cave, he is called a 'fell corpse'; if a man is hanged, he is called a 'gallows corpse'.
>
> *Grágás, Staðarhólsbók* 360 (cf. *Konungsbók, Baugatal* 113)

SACRIFICE AND LAW

At Windeby in northern Germany, the naked body of a teenage girl was held down in the bog with wooden hurdles and a large stone (*6*). She had been blindfolded and her hair was partially shaven. A few yards away lay the body of a man who had been strangled with a hazel branch. The Roman writer Tacitus tells us that sexual offenders were drowned in bogs and describes how an adulteress was stripped and shaved (*Germania* ch.12, 19). It is easy to assume that because these two bodies seem to represent punishment for an adulterous affair they cannot have been a religious sacrifice, but for the ancient Germans there seems to have been no clear distinction between judicial execution and sacrifice. Elsewhere in his study of the Germanic nations, Tacitus describes the process of law:

> Furthermore, no reprimands, no bonds nor yet beatings are allowed unless by the priests, not as punishment nor on a leader's orders, but as if on the god's command …
>
> *Germania*, ch.7

> Penalties are distinguished according to the crime. Traitors and deserters they hang from trees; idleness, cowardice and the sins of the flesh are plunged into the mud and mire under wicker hurdles.
>
> *Germania* ch.12

Although Tacitus describes criminals put to death by way of punishment, this does not exclude the possibility that their deaths were in some way sacrificial. Different penalties are matched with different crimes, and are not administered as punishment, but as religious devotion. The Icelandic *Kristni saga* states that 'the heathens sacrifice the very worst of men and push them over cliffs and precipices' (ch.7), while *Eyrbyggja saga* suggests that sacrifice was indeed used as a legal penalty.

It is not clear that any concept of fairness or justice was inherent in the choice of victim. In the tenth-century, Ibn Rusta witnessed similar power invested in the priests of the Rus, who seemed free to choose whoever they wanted for sacrifice; the Rus seem to have incorporated elements of both Scandinavian and Slavonic culture, but at this date the Scandinavian influence seems to have been dominant.

6 The body of the Windeby Girl from Schleswig-Holstein, Germany. She was shaved and blindfolded, before her body was pinned down in the bog with wooden hurdles and a heavy stone. *Stiftung Schleswig-Holsteinische Landesmuseen*

In some cases, even where the culprit was known, the victim seems to have been chosen by lot rather than by trial. Sacrifice is performed to pay for a crime, but the choice of victim does not necessarily involve what we would consider to be due legal process. Some victims must have been chosen as scapegoats, whose death might absolve the community of the taint of crime, but who could not be held responsible in any modern sense. Could the Windeby girl even have been a victim of rape, who was later sacrificed for her part in someone else's crime? This apparently arbitrary justice is at odds with the picture of a well-developed legal system that we find in later law codes or in the sagas, but probably reflects an equally trustworthy perspective on the reality of pre-Christian practice.

Perhaps law-breakers were given to the god they had offended. However, it seems more likely that, having offended against the laws of human society, they were sacrificed to the divinity who was associated with the sphere in which they had offended and who had thus already taken control of them on earth. Thus, sexual offences are punished by drowning, which might indicate sacrifice to the gods of the Vanir, such as the goddesses Freyja and Nerthus who ruled sexuality. It is as if Freyja has already chosen them as her own and her choice is revealed by their actions.

In this context, the line between punishment and sacrifice is very thin. If the Windeby couple were indeed adulterers, perhaps they were thought to have self-selected themselves for sacrifice.

OTHER HUMAN VICTIMS

Not all sacrifices can have been criminals. *Kristni saga*'s description of sacrificial victims as 'the worst of men' is open to a much wider interpretation. According to pathological evidence from the bog bodies, it certainly seems to have included people with physical deformities. Thus, the Yde girl suffered from a curved spine, the Kayhausen boy had a hip defect and the Huldremose woman limped due to a broken leg. Some archaeologists have suggested that their physical defects mean these victims would have been regarded as seers, but there is really no evidence that physical deformity (other than blindness) was ever seen as a mark of prophecy, and it is more likely that it was seen simply as a blight.

Yet if the supply of maimed or crippled victims and criminals should run out, there were always other potential sources. In AD 732, Pope Gregory II wrote to the missionary Boniface concerned that 'some of the faithful sell their slaves to be sacrificed by the heathen'. The Christian King Olaf Tryggvason is said to have taunted the people of Trondheim after killing their chieftain, saying that he doesn't just sacrifice their slaves and old men of no importance, but their wives and leaders too.

Slaves bought and sold for slaughter might still have been judged among the worst of men, but not all sacrifices were of such lowly status. A number of the best preserved bodies from the bogs, including Tollund man, were clearly not accustomed to manual labour in their lifetimes. *Ynglinga saga* tells of the sacrifice of the Swedish king Domaldi (ch.18), while *Gautreks saga* tells how King Vikar was sacrificed when lots were cast to find a victim (ch.7).

CHOICE BY LOT

Vikar is selected for sacrifice after the lots repeatedly point to him. He has commited no crime, but when his fleet is becalmed, divination reveals that Odin wishes for a sacrifice to be chosen by lot. In Alcuin's *Vita Willibrordi*, the King of Fositeland 'cast lots to find out who to sacrifice'. He does this nine times because he doesn't like the results; 'for three whole days he cast lots three times every day to find out who should die'. Likewise, Caesar recounts how the Roman envoy Valerius Procillus was held prisoner and lots were cast for who should die:

> He said that the lots were consulted three times about him in his presence, whether he should be killed at once by fire, or be kept back for another time; through the favour of the lots he was unharmed.
>
> *De Bello Gallico*, Bk 1 ch.53

The casting of lots to select victims for sacrifice deliberately embraces the random and arbitrary element which is so utterly at odds with legal justice. Casting lots allows for supernatural intervention in the process, so that the victims might seem to be chosen by the gods themselves. However, there was clearly provision for repeat consultations, if the gods did not at first give the looked-for answer.

Lots could also be used to select animals for sacrifice. Thus, Constantine Porphyrogenitos writes that when the Rus reached a certain island on the Dnieper where there was a gigantic oak tree, they went ashore to sacrifice cockerels at the tree; 'they also cast lots for the birds, whether to sacrifice them, or to eat them, or to let them live' (*De Administrando Imperio*). Adam of Bremen also considered lots to have been an important feature of pre-Christian Saxon religion (*Gesta Hammaburgensis*, Bk 1, ch.7-8).

According to Saxo, these lots took the form of 'three bits of wood, white on one side, black on the other, thrown into the lap' (Bk 2).

ANIMAL VICTIMS

> Then a horse was led forwards into the assembly and cut up and prepared for eating, and they reddened the tree of sacrifice with blood.
>
> *Hervarar saga ok Heiðreks*, ch.16

Most sacrificial victims were not people, but animals. Even at the great sacrifices held at Uppsala and Lejre, animals greatly outnumbered human victims. These were rare events, which took place only once every nine years; at other places and on other occasions, animals would have been offered alone.

Of animal victims, the bull and the horse seem to be mentioned most often, but sheep, goats, pigs, dogs and cockerels are also common. Pope Gregory observed that the Anglo-Saxons had 'a custom of sacrificing many oxen to demons' (Bede, *Historia Ecclesiastica* Book 1 ch.30). Certain animals might have been appropriate to particular gods, while others were more universally acceptable. The goats which draw Thor's wagon through the skies and the boar which carries Frey are probably the mythical counterparts of the offerings which were made to these gods by their followers.

After the slaughter, the meat was stewed so that the worshippers might share a feast with the gods. On Gotland, the co-worshippers called themselves 'stew-mates' (*suð-nautar*) because they ate the stewed meat together (*Gutalög, Guta saga* ch.1). In *Heimskringla*, King Olaf Tryggvason mocks the pagan Swedes, saying they would be better off at home 'licking their sacrifice bowls (*blótbolla*)' (*Ólafs saga Tryggvasonar* ch.112 (122)). The tenth-century Arab traveller Ibn Fadlan describes how among the Rus, after the beasts had been slaughtered and the food shared out, some of the carcass was offered before an upright wood stake, and the head was tied to its top. Likewise, Ibrahim al-Turtushi, a traveller from Moorish Spain who visited the Viking port of Hedeby in the mid-tenth century, described the sacrificial rites he saw there:

> They hold a feast at which they all gather to honour their god and to eat and drink. Whoever kills a beast as a sacrifice sets up a pole by the door of his house, and fastens the animal to it (whether bull, ram, he-goat or boar); thus the people know he has made an offering in honour of his god.
>
> Ibrahim ibn Ya'qub al-Turtushi, based on available translations

A remarkably full description of a sacrificial feast is found in an account by the thirteenth-century Icelandic historian Snorri Sturluson. We need to remember that this description was written long after the sacrifices it describes had ceased, and we cannot necessarily trust every detail, but while we might wish for a detailed eyewitness account, none has yet been discovered. As so often in matters of Scandinavian religion, Snorri is the best source we have, and although attempts have been made to discredit his testimony, there is nothing inherently incongruous in his account.

> It was the old custom when there was to be a sacrifice, that all the farmers would come to where the temple (*hof*) was, and bring their provisions there which they would have while the feast was on. At this feast, everyone had to have ale. All kinds of beasts were killed there and also horses. And all the blood which came out was then called '*hlaut*'. And they were '*hlaut*-bowls' which the blood stood in. '*hlaut*-twigs' which were made like sprinklers, which they would redden the altars with all over, and likewise the walls of the temple outside and in, and likewise they sprinkled it on the people. But the meat would be stewed for a banquet. The fire would be in the middle of the temple floor, and the cooking pots over it. And they would pass the toasting cup (*full*) across the fire. And he who gave the feast and was the headman, then he would bless the cup and all the meat of sacrifice. First was Odin's Toast, which he drank for victory and power to his king, and then Njörd's Toast and Frey's Toast for peace and plenty. Then it was the custom for many men to drink next the Chief Toast. People also drank toasts for their relations who had been buried, and that was called 'Remembrance'.
>
> *Heimskringla*, *Hákonar saga Aðalsteinsfóstra*, ch.14

It is not always easy for an archaeologist to tell the bones of sacrificial animals from those of any other slaughtered animal, but a large collection of ox skulls found at the site of an unusual building in the royal complex at Yeavering in England must represent the remains of sacrifice and it is probable that this building was used in sacrificial ritual.

HOARDS FROM THE BOGS

Sacrifices could also consist of inanimate objects. In 1858, Conrad Engelhardt began to excavate the bog of Thorsbjerg Mose in northern Germany, at the heart of the continental homeland of the Anglian nation, in Angeln. He discovered large deposits of pottery, mainly dating from before the second century AD. These pots will each have held some kind of sacrifice, usually a joint of meat, sometimes milk or butter. However, from the late second century a new style of offering takes the place of these homely sacrifices. Most striking are two Roman parade helmets, one of gilt silver. There are also Roman shields, swords, javelins, belts, armour and brooches; there are Germanic bows and arrows, shields, spears and horse fittings, and fine clothing – two pairs of trousers, two cloaks and a shirt. Many objects had been deliberately mutilated before they were thrown in the bog. Weapons had been bent or broken, shield bosses smashed and clothes had been slashed, but despite the wanton destruction, there was a sense of order in the offerings – the shields were neatly stacked, the arrows bundled together. The last major deposit of war-gear was made here in the third century.

In another bog hoard from Vimose on the Danish island of Fyn, the earliest offerings are of pots of food, but during the Roman period, there are offerings of weapons and armour, dating mostly from the late second and early third centuries, alongside tools, brooches and wooden tubs. A similar selection of offerings was found at Nydam in Denmark, a site which was used from the second century onwards. Here the magnificence of the weaponry, which included over a hundred swords (most of them pattern-welded) and nearly 600 spears, was enhanced by the ships which bore it. Of three ships, only two have been excavated, one of which dates to the second century and the other to the fourth. A Norwegian bog ship from Kvalsund dates from the Migration era or even later.

Other major bog deposits from the Roman Iron Age and later have been found at Ejsbøl, Illerup and Kragehul in Denmark, and Skedemosse in Sweden. Most of these thrived in the third and fourth centuries AD, though the earliest deposits are from as early as the second century BC and the latest are from the sixth century AD. None of these sites seems to have lasted throughout this period, and some, such as Illerup, might have been used for only a couple of hundred years. Finds at such sites typically include massive quantities of animal bone. Most often these are the bones from the tail and feet along with the skull; the rest has gone to make the meal, with bones perhaps used for the cooking fire, bonfire or 'bone fire'. There are also huge numbers of pots which would once have held food, and sometimes still contain identifiable animal remains; these simple gifts of food seem to have been quite distinct from offerings of live animals. Other offerings included clothing and tools, as well as the magnificent caches of weapons and armour.

The weapons and armour found in these sacrificial bogs were probably the spoils of war. The destruction of enemy treasures by the warriors of the Cimbri and Teutoni is vividly described by Orosius:

> The enemy took both camps, and a vast amount of booty. Following a strange and unusual vow, they proceeded to destroy all that they had gained. Clothing was torn up and thrown away, gold and silver dumped in the river, men's armour broken up, horse fittings wrecked, the horses themselves drowned in the streams; people were hanged from the trees with ropes round their necks.
>
> *Historiæ*, Bk 5 ch.16

A similar battle vow is recorded by Tacitus:

> The war brought success to the Hermunduri, ruin to the Chatti, because they had offered the opposing army to Mars or Mercury if they won, a vow which sends horses, men, every living thing to destruction, and indeed their hostile threats turned against them.
>
> *Annales*, Bk 13 ch.57

The hanging of 111 Frankish prisoners at Charlevanne (now part of Paris) by the Viking leader Ragnar Lodbrok has been seen as a late example of the same practice, as has Ongentheow's threat to hang his captives in the Anglo-Saxon poem *Beowulf* (l.2940-1).

Such mass sacrifices were probably deposited not only in bogs, but at other holy sites too. However, bog deposits have survived better than more obvious and lootable hoards. In his *De Bello Gallico*, Caesar describes a similar tradition among the Gauls:

> When they choose to give battle, they usually consecrate the spoils of war to Mars. Having won, they sacrifice the captured animals, and gather the remaining things in one place. In many communities, you may see mounds built of these things in holy places ...
>
> *De Bello Gallico*, Bk 6 ch.17

The predilection for war gear may have fallen off in the fourth century, but the tradition of leaving heaps of wealth as religious offerings continued into the Vendel era if not later. The *Annals of the Frankish Kings* record that Charlemagne took gold and silver from the shrine of the Saxon Irminsul, and the *Vita Liudgeri* also records that Liudger took treasure from Saxon temples (ch.14). Not all donations to these sacred hoards need have been the spoils of war. In the medieval romance *Örvar-Odds saga*, the Perms are said have a sacred mound, where they leave a handful of silver whenever someone dies and a handful of earth when someone is born.

HOMELIER OFFERINGS

It is easy to become diverted by the glamour of live sacrifice, ships and war gear from the fact that many sacrificial offerings appear to have been far more mundane in character. Other offerings included joints of meat, bundles of flax, and apparently animal fat.

In the Icelandic *Landnámabók*, the settler Thorstein Rednose is said to have worshipped a waterfall with gifts of food, while in *Hauksbók* some women were apparently still in the habit of taking food to pillars and caves, where they would 'consecrate it to the land-spirits and then eat it'. The Byzantine emperor-author Constantine Porphyrogenitus writes that the Rus made offerings of bread and meat, as well as live birds (*De Administrando Imperio*, *c*.950). Similarly, Ibn Fadlan tells how they take bread, meat, onions, milk and alcohol as offerings to a tall pole with a face like a man's. The ubiquitous broken pots that litter sacrificial sites will once have contained food offerings.

The Anglo-Saxon charm 'Land remedy', which contains both Christian and pre-Christian elements, calls for a loaf of bread to be ploughed into the ground, with an invocation for fertility: 'Then take every kind of flour, and have a palm-sized loaf of bread baked, and knead it with milk and with holy water, and lay it under the first furrow.' In Upper Banffshire, Scotland, the ritual of placing a cake of specially baked bread under the first furrow was kept until the nineteenth century.

Farm tools seem to have been significant in votive deposits at Thorsbjerg, Nydam and Rappendam in Denmark, and at Käringsjön in Sweden, where ploughshares were associated with wagon parts and wheels. At Oberdorla in Germany, pottery, tools and wheels were found alongside the bones of many animals and at least 40 people. At Forlev Nymølle, bundles of flax had been offered along with pottery and bones (from joints of meat) to a branch roughly shaped as a woman, and at Käringsjön they lay alongside farm implements, bones and traces of animal fat.

CHAPTER 2
INVOCATION

PRAYER

All sacrifices must have been offered with prayers, but it is only very rarely that we catch their echo. A remarkable, if somewhat cynical account of a Rus merchant at prayer was recorded by Ibn Fadlan. The merchant approaches a wooden idol with offerings for sacrifice:

> [When] he reaches the large figure, he prostrates himself before it and says, 'Lord, I have come from a distant land, bringing so many slave-girls [priced] at such and such per head and so many sables [priced] at such and such per pelt.' He continues until he has mentioned all of the merchandise he has brought with him, then says, 'And I have brought this offering,' leaving what he has brought with him in front of the piece of wood, saying, 'I wish you to provide me with a merchant who has many dīnārs and dirhams and who will buy from me whatever I want [to sell] without haggling over the price I fix.' Then he departs.
>
> (Montgomery's translation)

The prayer of Thorkell the High of Thverá is based on a similar formula (*Víga Glúms saga* ch.9): 'Frey, he said, who has long been my "full-trusty" and received many gifts from me and repaid them well, now I give you this ox to this end …' He begins by reminding the god of their past relationship and mutual gifts, before offering a new gift with a specific object in mind, in this case to drive his adversary Glum from the land. In both cases, the purpose of prayer and sacrifice can be expressed by the Latin tag *do ut des*, 'I give that you might give', or, as the poet of *Hávamál* puts it, 'A gift demands a return' (st.144).

Poetic prayer appears to have been considered especially potent. The Anglo-Saxon 'Land Remedy' is one of a number of poetic charms from all areas of the Germanic world, and fragments of hymns in praise of Thor still survive, which refer to his mythical victories. In the medieval Icelandic *Eiríks saga rauða*, Thorhall recites a poem he has made for his god Thor (ch.8). Another surviving poetic invocation takes the form of a straightforward salutation, to which various specific prayers might be appended according to the occasion:

> Hail the day! Hail sons of the day!
> Hail the night and her kin!
> With peaceable eyes may you look upon us,
> And give victory to those who sit here.
>
> Hail the gods! Hail the goddesses!
> Hail the full-fruitful earth!
> Words and wit may you give us both,
> And healing hands while we live.
>
> *Sigrdrífumál*, st.3-4

Prayers for the future could sometimes be accompanied by sacrifices and sacrifice could also be offered after the event, as thanksgiving. Thus, if business was brisk for Ibn Fadlan's merchant, he would make another offering when he has finished trading, saying, 'My Lord has satisfied my request, so I am required to recompense him' (Montgomery's translation).

In *Vita Anskarii*, which describes the apostle Anskar's mission to Sweden in the ninth century, the hard-pressed Swedes are unable to offer immediate sacrifice, but promise future offerings to their gods in return for their lives (ch.19). In the medieval Icelandic *Egils saga*, a formal duel or *hólmganga* is arranged between two adversaries, and although the victim is prepared before the duel takes place, it is only the victor who makes sacrifice: 'A bull was led out, big and old. It was called the "sacrificial beast"; whoever took the victory would kill it. Sometimes it was one beast, sometimes each of the duellers led out his own' (ch.66). In this case, Egill wins the fight and slaughters the bull.

The Rus merchant described by Ibn Fadlan prostrates himself before his wooden idol when he prays, and similar depictions of obeisance in the presence of the divine can be found in other sources. Tacitus writes of the holy grove of the Semnones that 'No one goes in unless tied in bonds, as a minion before the power of the divinity. If he happens to stumble, he is forbidden to get up or to be lifted up; he must roll along the ground' (*Germania* ch.39).

In the saga of the Norwegian King Olaf the Holy, *Olafs saga helga*, Dala-Gudbrand's followers bow down before a statue of Thor (ch.113). However, Thorhall seems to adopt a different position for his prayers to Thor in *Eiríks saga rauða*. His companions discover him on a clifftop: 'He was lying there looking up in the air with his mouth wide open and his nostrils flared, reciting' (ch.8). Likewise, Tacitus describes prayers offered while looking up to heaven (*Germania*, ch.10).

A very different impression is made by a burlesque episode in the saga of King Olaf Tryggvason known as *Völsa þáttr*. The missionary king has sought lodging with a peasant household, far from the hub of his kingdom. Here the household venerate 'Völsi', a preserved horse's phallus, which they pass between them around the room, as each recites a verse in Völsi's honour. Some of the verses are distinctly libidinous and they are sometimes accompanied by actions to match. Whilst this story appears to be an absurd lampoon, it is unlikely to be utterly without foundation in truth.

The semi-Christainised Anglo-Saxon 'Land remedy' cited above, also involves a combination of ritual action and invocation:

> A man should take unknown seed from beggars and give them twice as much as he took from them, and gather all his plough gear together ... Then take that seed, set it on the plough's beam, and say:
> 'Erce, Erce, Erce, mother of earth, may the All-ruler, the eternal Lord, grant you fields growing and sprouting, greatening and strengthening, tall stalks, adorning crops and broad barley crops and white wheat crops and all earth's crops ...'
> Then, when the man drives forth the plough and cuts the first furrow, say:
> 'Health to you, Earth, mother of men! Be growing in God's embrace, filled with food for the needs of men.'

OATHS, CURSES AND BLESSINGS

The counterparts of prayer are vows, blessings and curses. Without a single monotheistic power to impose a single set of commandments, supernatural moral sanction existed through oath-taking. These oaths could be sworn by any number of sacred or useful objects, the idea being that these would turn against the oath-taker if he should break his word. In the poem *Völundarkviða* which was possibly composed in Viking York, oaths are sworn by the ship's side, the shield's rim, the horse's back and the blade's edge. Vows pledged on a holy object or by a divine power have always been thought especially binding. Thus, the eighth-century English *Liber Pœnitentialis* seeks to end the use of pre-Christian holy sites for oath-taking, stating 'If anyone should make a vow at trees, or at springs, or at stones, or else at fences ... this is sacrilege, that is worship of demons'.

A particular form of sacred vow known from Viking Scandinavia was taken on a holy ring. According to *Eyrbyggja saga* and *Landnámabók*, such a ring was kept in every temple and had by law to conform to a certain standard weight. In the ninth-century poem *Atlakviða*, Atli is reminded of the oath he has sworn 'by the ring of Ullr' amongst other oaths. The Icelandic *Landnámabók* gives a possible formula for swearing such an oath, describing how a man undertaking legal business at the assembly had to swear to three gods on a sacred ring at the temple, with the words 'I name … as witness, that I take an oath at the ring, a law oath, so help me Frey and Njörd and the almighty god …'. Such rings could apparently have specific histories and local political associations. Thus, the Irish *Annals of the Four Masters* say that 'the ring of Tomar' was looted from the temple in Dublin by King Maelseachlainn in 994; Tomar appears in earlier annals as a Viking war leader, but his ring had probably come to be venerated as a relic. Similarly, the ring known as the 'Swedes' Piglet' (*svía-gríss*) which was taken by King Hrolf from the Swedish court was said to have belonged to the ancestors of the Swedish kings and must have been important as a national totem.

Not all oaths were to be trusted. Oaths in the poem *Atlakviða* have already been broken when they are listed, and oaths are broken in the pre-Christian Icelandic poem *Völuspá* too. Odin's untrustworthiness is alluded to in *Hávamál*, which derisively suggests he must have sworn a ring oath when he betrayed the giant Suttung. Perhaps it was by Odin that the Danes swore in 876, when according to the *Anglo-Saxon Chronicle*, they 'swore oaths to King Alfred upon the holy ring, which before they would not do … and which by night they broke'.

The vows we have so far considered stand as promises of good conduct, truth or friendship. However, there was another kind of vow: a solemn promise to undertake a feat. By such an oath, one bound oneself to accomplish a given task, and in so doing, apparently bound in the help of the god.

In the Icelandic *Jómsvíkinga saga*, oaths like this are made at the Yule feast, which marked the turning of the year. As such, these vows could be the ancestors of the modern New Year's Resolution, but rather than looking towards moral improvement, the Yule pledge was usually a commitment to worldly advancement. The Anglo-Saxon poem known as 'The Wanderer', although overtly Christian, recalls this ancient custom in its advice to the hero, that he should fully know his mind before he swears such a vow (l.70-2). The Jomsvikings swear unwisely, and bring down disaster on themselves.

The religious component of such a vow appears to have been that, as the worshipper shares his meal with the god, so the god will help him to make good his vow. This tradition perhaps allowed worshippers to piggyback their own individual prayers on the communal sacrifice. While the patron offered sacrifice on behalf of the community and asked for favour in return, the oath-taker who swore on the living victim ensured that, just as the god accepted the offering so he must also accept his part in the offered pledge.

Vows taken in *Beowulf* seem to offer future sacrifice in exchange for immediate help. Here the phrase 'praying with words' (*wordum bædon*) could suggest that such vows were seen as a form of offering in themselves, as an alternative to praying with sacrifice.

> For the time they took vows at shrine shelters
> in honour of idols, praying with words
> that the Soul-slayer should send them succour
> against the nation's troubles.
>
> *Beowulf*, l. 175-8

A remarkable curse known as *Buslubæn* is included in the fourteenth-century narrative of *Bosa saga*. In its current form, it is not ancient, but it does follow what might be an ancient pattern for such curses. Thus, just as in *Völundarkviða* an oath is sworn by the ship's side, so *Buslubæn* calls on it to break, and just as in *Atlakviða*, an oath by 'rest bed's mount', *Buslubæn* calls on the bed to break too.

However, Skirnir's curse in the poem *Skirnismál* is rather different, as is Egil's curse on King Eirik Bloodaxe in *Egils saga* (ch.56, 57). Each of these involves some magical apparatus. *Skirnismál* is a mythological poem which is generally dated to the Viking Age, although the age of some of the verses of this curse has recently been called into question. In it, the mythical Skirnir relies on his 'taming wand' (*tams-vöndr*, st.26), while in *Egils saga*, Egil sets up a 'scorn post' (*níð-stöng*). This scorn post is a hazel rod topped with a horse's head and it is perhaps intended as an inverted sacrifice; having already cursed the king in verse, Egil now curses the land spirits that they must go astray until they drive Eirik and his queen from the land. Another scorn post is set up by Jökul in *Vatnsdæla saga*:

> ... they took a pole and carried it into the yard ... Jökul carved a man's head on the end of the pole and wrote in runes all the clauses which were said before. Then Jökul killed a mare and opened her at the breast and offered her on the pole, and he made it turn towards Borg.
>
> *Vatnsdæla saga* ch.34

Like Egil's post, Jökul's is put up as a sanction against someone who is judged to be in contempt of the law; Egil's post is raised against King Eirik Bloodaxe, when he 'defiles the assembly' by breaking down the sanctuary ropes, while Jökul's is raised against Berg and Finnbogi, when they fail to appear for a legal duel. As such, both scorn posts are announced in the assembly before they are set up. Also like Egil's post, Jökul's not only invokes the wrath of the gods against his enemies, but also names them as law-breakers (*Egils saga*, ch.56; *Vatnsdæla saga*, ch.33).

Very likely, blessings played a greater part in everyday life than did curses and vows, but they do not feature heavily in literature. The Anglo-Saxon 'Land remedy' quoted below, though in effect a prayer for a good harvest, is couched in the form of a blessing on the earth. The final verse of the poem *Hávamál* invokes a blessing on anyone who speaks it, knows it, learns it or listens to it (st.164). A little runic amulet in the shape of a fish from Kvinneby on the Swedish island of Öland, is inscribed with a blessing for one Bofi. The full text is open to various interpretations, but its general meaning is clear. Amongst other more obscure lines it says, 'May Thor protect him with that hammer … The gods are below him and above him'. Finally an ephemeral blessing survives on a rune stick from Viking Bergen, which reads, 'Be healthy and in good spirit: May Thor receive you; may Odin keep you.'

RITUAL GAMES

Besides prayers and curses, there were other ways for pre-Christian worshippers to invoke the gods. In Thorbjörn Hornklofi's tenth-century poem *Haraldskvæði*, the Viking celebration of Yule includes the playing of a game dedicated to the god Frey (*Freys leikr*, st.6). In fact, the meaning of the Norse word *leikr* is somewhat wider than the Modern English 'game' and it includes dramatic performances as well as sports and contests, but it does seem that pre-Christian celebrations could be decidedly 'playful'. Games are held at the festival of Winter's Eve in *Eyrbyggja saga*, *Víga-Glúms saga* and *Gísla saga*, and Yule games are played in *Hauks þáttr hábrókar* and *Laxdæla saga*. These are usually ball games, wrestling and swimming.

The Anglo-Saxon *Canons of Edgar* takes a dim view of such entertainments, calling for an end to 'the holidays of the heathen people and games of the devil'. Similar 'games of the devil' along with 'wicked dancing' and 'other superstitions' were once held by Erchinoald's Frankish household at Noyon in Picardie, who described them as 'our time-honoured and beloved games' (*Vita Eligii*, Bk 2 ch.20).

The second day of Christmas is still kept as a sports day in many countries up to the present time. In England it is celebrated with football matches, horse racing and hunts on horseback. In Scandinavia, the second day of Christmas was also traditionally celebrated with horse races, with neighbouring farms competing to reach a north-flowing spring, where the winner would cast a silver coin into the water before allowing his the horse to drink (7). These modern winter sports are perhaps surviving relics of Frey's games.

The Norse word *skeið*, meaning 'horse race, racecourse', features in place names across Norway and Sweden. Most of the farms named after these horse races stand at or near likely pre-Christian cult sites. One such site is at Skedemosse on Öland,

7 Illustration of the traditional Scandinavian horse race held on St Stephen's Day, the second day of Christmas. *From* Historia de gentibus, *Olaus Magnus*

where the peat has yielded evidence of a major cult site which operated between the third and sixth centuries. Finds included a great number of horse bones from more than a hundred separate animals, as well as many horse trappings. Other animals were also sacrificed here, including cattle and goats, but horse bones represent as much 35 per cent of the total assemblage. Horses also feature prominently in the sacrifice at Hlaðir described in *Hákonar saga*, and there might well have been races or horse fights before the sacrifice here too.

Horse fighting is frequently mentioned in the sagas, and remained popular in parts of Scandinavia long after the advent of Christianity, but as Terry Gunnell has shown, it did not shed its association with the old religion. In 1592, for instance, the Icelandic Bishop Oddur Einarsson banned priests from 'horse fights, vigils, gatherings of common people and shepherds, and other relics of pagan ceremony'. In Telemark, where a good horse fight was said to foretell a good year, a horse that died in the ring was buried where it fell together with its trappings. According to the Olaus Magnus, in sixteenth-century Sweden, the winning horse was sacrificed to the gods (*Historia de gentibus* Bk 1 ch.24). In many parts of northern Europe including Anglo-Saxon England, stallions were sometimes buried in their own grave, often with their harness as grave goods. Are these, one wonders, the graves of the unlucky winners?

MASKED MEN AND SEVERED HEADS

Among the finds from the harbour silts of Hedeby were two animal masks of heavy felt (*8*). One has been interpreted as a cow and the other as a sheep, although other interpretations are possible. The 'cow' mask would have covered the wearer's whole face, while the 'sheep' mask would have covered only the upper face. Very probably, these masks would have been used in a ritual performance.

The seventh-century *Penitential* of Archbishop Theodore of Canterbury forbids people from celebrating the New Year by dressing in the heads and skins of stags and cattle (ch.27). Men wearing horns and animal masks appeared on the ceremonial golden horns from Gallehus in Denmark, while a female figure with pig's head and drum appears on the ninth-century Norwegian tapestry from Oseberg, as does a female figure with a bird's head. Dancers at Abbots Bromley in England use reindeer antlers which have been carbon dated to the eleventh century.

A description of a Byzantine court ritual sheds an interesting sidelight on these masked guisers. In his book *De cerimoniis aulae Byzantiae*, the tenth-century emperor Constantine Porphyrogenitus described a dance performed for him by the 'Goths' of his Varangian Guard (Bk 1 ch.23). In his day, the Guard was made up of Scandinavians and Rus rather than Goths, but the curious ritual of the

8 Felt mask from Hedeby in the form of an animal head (Fragment 25), possibly a cow or calf

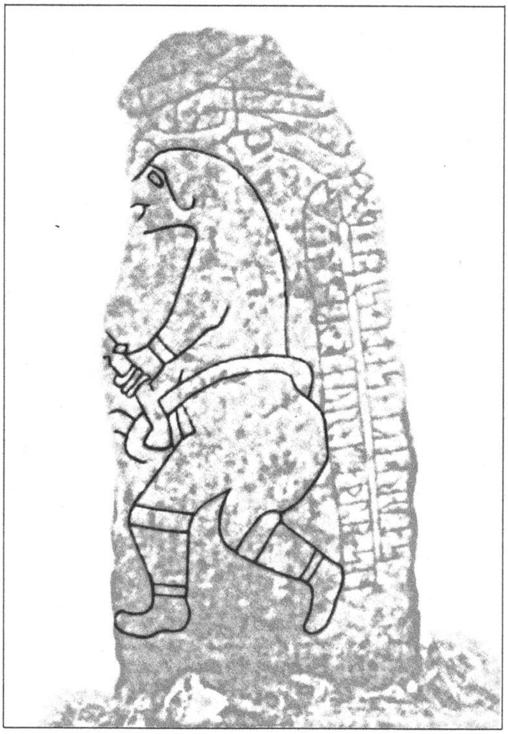

9 This image of an animal guiser from a runic stone at Källby (Västergötland, Sweden) seems to be wearing a mask similar to those from Viking Hedeby

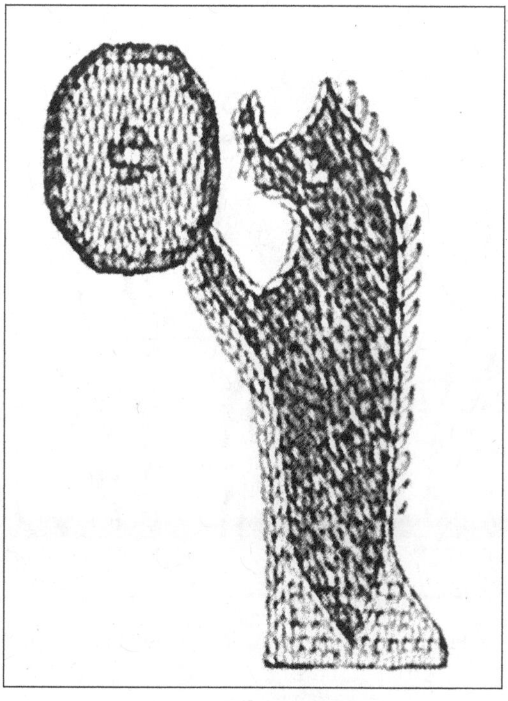

10 This figure from the Oseberg Tapestry seems to show a woman in the skin of a pig. *Based on an illustration by M. Storm*

11 Another figure from the Oseberg Tapestry represents a woman dressed as a bird. *After Sofie Krafft*

12 Figures from one of the lost golden horns from Gallehus, Denmark, dated to the fifth century

Gothikon probably has earlier roots. According to Porphyrogenitus, on the ninth day of Chistmas, sailors and guardsmen would dance around the emperor at his table. The dancers formed two groups, led by their military commanders. They were accompanied by musicians and each group included a pair of 'Goths', dressed in masks and animal skins. They would rush in, banging their shields loudly and shouting '*Toúl! Toúl!*', until they reached the emperor's table where they formed a double circle, and with one group dancing inside the other, they danced three times around the table. The 'Goths' then began an oration in praise of the emperor. The oration is a strange accretion of elements in several languages including Gothic, Latin, Hebrew and Greek, but the core of the ritual looks ancient, and is very probably Germanic.

Hard evidence linking modern traditions with earlier practice is often rather slight, but the guising character Grýla clearly goes back at least to the thirteenth century. Grýla is a troll wife, who still visits households in the Faroes at Shrovetide, introducing herself with the words, 'Down comes Grýla from the yard with forty tails …'. A verse in the medieval Icelandic *Sturlunga saga* contains the words, 'Here comes Grýla down into the yard, and on her she has fifteen tails!' Although she is now associated with a Christian festival, there is no obvious Christian origin for Grýla and it is very likely that she has an earlier pre-Christian origin. However, as so often in these guising rituals, the most important element seems to be dramatic rather than symbolic.

Modern Scandinavian Yuletude guising traditions often involve horned figures, reminiscent of those described in Theodore's *Penitential*. The most notable of these is the *julebukk* (or *julegeit*), the 'Yule Goat'. The performer is dressed in skins, and either wears the horns on his head or holds up a horned head on a stick as a 'pole-goat'. At Bergen, a 'father' and 'son' lead in the Yule Goat and sing about how they slaughter the goat and sell its hide, its wool, its beard, its legs and so on, until they have sold the lot, when the goat comes back to life.

> The goat stands up and shakes his beard –
> He hopped and he sprang on the floor!

In very many such traditional Yule games, including the traditional English Mummers' Plays, the action revolves around the death and resurrection of the animal or another character. In the case of the *julebukk*, the guising animal might represent the real goat which was once eaten for Christmas dinner. In Setesdal, the animal killed for Yule celebrations was traditionally fed on the last sheaf of corn and was called the *julebukk*. Traditional Scandinavian children's games noted by Gunnell in this connection include 'Slaughtering the Goat' (*Slakta bocken*) and 'Blowing life into the dead goat' (*Blåsa liv in den daude bukken*).

13 Die for a helmet plaque from Torslunda (Öland, Sweden), showing a near-naked dancing man and another dressed in a wolfskin

14 Animal-headed figure on a plaque from Gutenstein near Sigmaringen (Baden-Württemberg, Germany)

15 Seated animal-headed figure on the Northumbrian 'Franks Casket'. It is usually dated to the seventh century and includes legendary as well as Christian scenes. The runic text associated with this picture may be rendered 'The idol god sits on the hill of harm'. To the right of the horse, a standing figure stands in the same relation to a smaller figure as in the sacrificial scene from Lärbro Stora Hammars (*2*)

The English song 'The Derby Ram' clearly forms part of the same tradition as the Bergen *julebukk* song. This song, which is sung to accompany the death of 'Old Tup', also tells how the animal is slaughtered and lists its various parts, describing how some are disposed of; Old Tup is represented by a man hidden under a sack with a ram's head held aloft on a broomstick. A German and Austrian equivalent is known as *Habergeis* or *Habergaiss*, the 'Oat Goat'.

In England, the guising animal is more often a horse than a sheep or goat. Hobby horses of all kinds are known from all over England (including the popular pantomime horse), but in some places, as at Antrobus in Cheshire and Ramsgate in Kent, it takes the form of a pole horse, with a real horse's head or skull mounted on a stick. Occasional Scandinavian references, including an early fourteenth-century reference to 'Arnold the Christmas Horse' (*Arnaldus Jolahest*) show that a 'hobby horse' tradition once existed in Scandinavia too (*Diplomatorium Norvegicum*, VIII 29).

The use of a real animal head mounted on a stick is strikingly reminiscent of the sacrificial rituals described above, where the victim's head is set upon a pole. Even more strikingly, a ceremony almost identical to the rites of the *julebukk* and his kin was performed in the sixth century by the Langobards in northern Italy.

> At the same time, while the Langobards were holding nearly four hundred prisoners, they sacrificed a goat's head to the devil according to their custom,

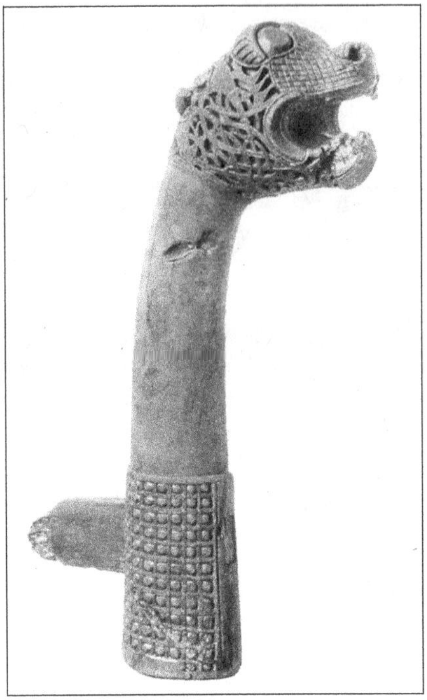

16 One of the animal-headed posts from the Oseberg burial. Each had what looks like a handle, at right angles to the post. If carried by an appropriately disguised performer, it could have appeared rather like the animal-headed figure on the Franks Casket (*15*)

> running round with it in a circle and hallowing it with an unspeakable song. And when with bowed necks they had first worshipped it themselves, they forced the prisoners to worship it too.
>
> Gregory the Great, *Dialogues*, Bk 3 ch.28

This adoration of a real fresh goat's head is very reminiscent of the *julebukk*. In modern tradition, the head of the newly-sacrificed animal might be replaced with a head made of wood, or by an ancient skull, but the connection is clear. Although this description is unusual in giving details of the pole-goat's dance, in other respects, this seems to have been a typical sacrifice. Gregory's account tells how, on the same occasion, the Langobards attempted to make their captives eat the meat of sacrificial animals (ch.27). It seems likely that similar dances would have formed a common feature of sacrificial rituals across the Germanic world.

Gregory is conspicuously evasive about the content of the Langobard song, calling it 'unspeakable' (*nefandus*). Similarly, in his description of the sacrifice at Uppsala, Adam of Bremen closes his vivid account of the sacrifice with the words, 'However, the dirges which are customarily performed in a libation rite of this kind are many and shameful, and so it is better to say no more'. We might detect a similar unease behind Saxo's allusions to the rites at Uppsala, or Bede's mention of the Anglo-Saxon celebration of Modranicht.

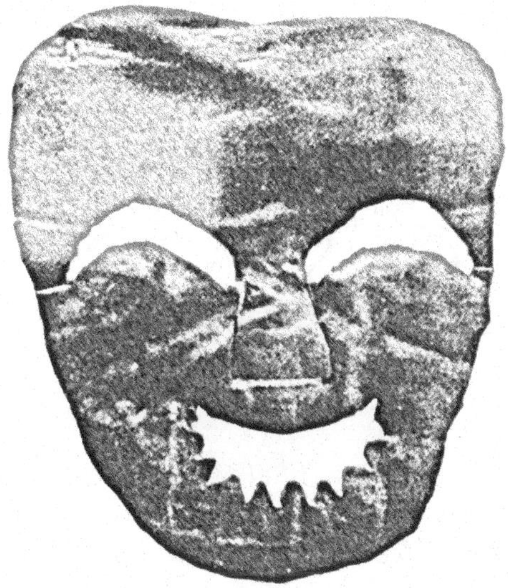

17 Leather mask from medieval Novgorod. Similar masks could have disguised non-animal performers in the ritual games

What then is the nature of this pagan sacrificial song, which the old authors will not reveal? Perhaps, a version of the song might still be sung today in Britain and Norway, since it need not have differed greatly from its modern descendants such as the song of the Bergen *julebukk* quoted above. Though its modern descendants might seem fairly banal, within the context of a sacrificial ceremony such a song would resonate with religious meaning. It is the song which claims that the dead shall live again. As well as being the theme of these traditional accompaniments to guising animals, this is the meaning of the myths of Thor's goats and of Frey's boar, divine animals which can be eaten in the evening and yet be alive and well in the morning. Just so, in the pre-Christian world, sacrifice offered on earth may be understood to live with the gods. In myth, the meat from Thor's goats is shared with his mortal hosts, just as the sacrificial meal is shared by the host with the god. The goat given to Thor in this world becomes the goat which draws his wagon among the gods.

This is the one theme which would be anathema to Christian writers, for it would claim that any sacrificial animal could be resurrected in the name of whatever god it might have been dedicated to. This strikes right at the heart of Christian belief, denying the uniqueness of the sacrifice of Jesus on the cross. For a pious medieval Christian, this would amount to the most scurrilous blasphemy. Such a song would indeed be considered unrepeatable.

The head mounted on a stick is, as we have seen, part of wider sacrificial traditions; what is remarkable about Gregory's account is that the head is paraded like a *julebukk*. This represents the reanimation of the sacrificial animal, which is also the meaning of the accompanying songs.

CHAPTER 3
GODS, GROVES AND IDOLS

Tacitus claimed that the Germanic peoples did not use temples, not thinking it fitting to 'confine the gods within walls, nor liken them to any human appearance', but that they worshipped outdoors in sacred woods and groves (*Germania*, ch.9). The question of temples is in fact rather more complicated than this, but for Tacitus at least, the focus of Germanic worship was very much in the natural world.

A similar impression is given by the numerous laws and decretals written to suppress old forms of religious worship after the introduction of Christianity. These speak of worship at trees, groves, wells, stones, fences and cairns (*18*). The eighth-century *Indiculus superstitionum et paganiarum* speaks of 'the woodland worship which they call *nimidas*', of 'those things which they do upon stones', and of 'the spring wells of sacrifice' (*Indiculus* 6, 7, 11). The Carolingian legal text *Capitulatio de partibus saxoniae* also legislates against worship at wells, trees and groves.

At Uppsala in Sweden, ritual activity was focused on a grove, which Adam of Bremen says was 'so holy that each tree is itself regarded as sacred', and a later addition to Adam's account describes 'a huge tree, which stretches out green branches in summer and winter alike; of what species nobody knows. There is also a spring there at which pagan sacrifices take place …' (*Gesta Hammaburgenis*, Bk 4 ch.26 *schol.*134). Adam also attributes worship of trees and springs to the pre-Christian Saxons (Bk 1 ch.8).

A number of English sources speak of the same kinds of sacred sites. Thus, for instance, the *Canons of Wulfstan* forbids 'well worship … and [worship] at sanctuaries and at elder trees and also at various other trees and at stones …', while an eleventh-century English translation of Haltigar's *Penitential* states:

> Some people are so blinded that they bring their offerings to an earth-fast stone and also to trees and well springs …

This passage suggests that the tree, well or stone is the object of worship in itself. The same assumption is found in Willibald's *Vita Bonifatii*, where the saint

18 A sacred birch tree at Slinde (Sogn og Fjordane, Norway). Until it fell in 1874, no one was allowed to cut its branches and every Christmas the farmer's family poured ale over its roots. *Painted in 1840 by Thomas Fearnley*

discovers that '... some continued secretly, others openly, to offer sacrifices to trees and springs ...' This would seem to suggest that worship was largely based around very localised animistic cults, rooted entirely in the immediate landscape. However, many sources, beginning with Tacitus, suggest that the physical place of worship is merely a focus for the presence of the universal gods.

Tacitus clearly understood the natural sanctuaries of *Germania* to be sacred to numinous powers, where 'they apply the names of deities to that hidden presence seen only by the eye of reverence' (*Germania*, ch.9). He writes that the Semnones believe their sacred grove to be the home of the all-powerful god who rules over others (Germania, ch.39), and in his *Annales*, he records a fierce war fought over a sacred river between the Hermunduri and the Chatti, who held 'an inborn belief that such places are nearest to heaven, and nowhere are mortal prayers better heard by the gods' (Bk 13 ch.57).

Clearly, different places or natural features might have been sacred to different divinities. An oak tree sacred to the thunder god was encountered by the missionary Boniface, who 'at a place called Gaesmere, attempted to fell a certain oak of extraordinary size, which to the ancient pagans was called by the name "Jove's Oak"'; when the oak was felled, he used the wood to build a Christian oratory. This episode is closely mirrored by archaeological information from Hov on the island of Frösö in Lake Storsjön, Sweden. Here, under the altar of a medieval church was found the stump of a large birch tree, about 20in wide (50cm), surrounded by animal bones including the remains of bears, elks, stags, goats (or sheep), pigs and cows. These animals had apparently been hung in the tree, just like the victims at Uppsala. Nearby stood two large grave mounds. The name Hov probably means 'temple', while Frösö means 'Frey's Isle', so like the holy grove at Uppsala, this site had been sacred to Frey. Radiocarbon dating suggests that this shrine flourished in the tenth century and was destroyed in the eleventh, when Frey's Birch was felled and replaced with a Christian church, just as Jove's Oak had been.

On an island in the Dnieper, there once stood a massive oak tree like that felled by Boniface, and the tenth-century emperor Constantine Porphyrogenitus tells how, as Rus merchants made their way downriver, they would stop and make offerings there (*De Administrando Imperio*). Perhaps, this tree too was dedicated to the thunder god. A similar island sanctuary may have stood at Torsholma on the Swedish island of Helgö. Torsholma means 'Thor's Island', and Helgö, which means 'Holy Isle', lies in the River Helgå, or 'Holy River'. It might be significant that Helgö is a river island, since rivers often feature in myths about Thor.

Wells also feature in accounts of Germanic holy places. The missionary Willibrord went to an island called Fositeland on the border between the Frisians and Danes, which was sacred to the god Fosite. As well as 'temples' and sacred cattle, the island was distinguished by a holy spring (*Vita Willibrordi*). Worship at 'water wells' was specifically prohibited by the laws of Cnut and the *Indiculus superstitionum et paganiarum* notes 'sacrificial spring wells'. Such a sacrificial well is also said to have existed at Uppsala, where it was probably sacred to Frey.

Clearly the trees at Gaesmere and Frösö are holy trees, but in their holiness the individual trees are each associated with a universal god; other objects and places are similarly associated with specific named gods. Wooden idols in bogs allow us to identify these sacred sites with personalised divinities, even if we do not know their names. The locality or object of veneration is not powerful in and of itself, but is a pathway to the same universal gods we know from written sources. The particular partakes of the universal.

Place names from England and Scandinavia seem to confirm this picture, regularly combining the name of a god with a natural feature, very often a grove. Anglo-Saxon worship in sacred groves is probably reflected in place names such as the English Thunderley ('Thunor's Grove') and Tuesley ('Tiw's Grove'). Likewise in Scandinavia, we find names such as Torslund or Thorlund ('Thor's Grove') and Tislund ('Tyr's Grove'). Lakes and hills are associated with gods at Odensjö ('Odin's lake'), Helganäs ('Holy headland'), Vibjerg (modern Viborg, 'Holy mount'), and at Wuodensberg (now Godesberg, 'Woden's mount') in Germany.

There is a kind of seamless continuity from bog to lake to well, from grove to tree, from earth-fast stone to wooden pillar to carved pillar to crude idol, which seems to show that all these different kinds of sacred object are just different expressions of the same idea. They all reveal the same basic principle that a god can take on a physical presence in the real world.

Unsurprisingly perhaps, the various types of sacred site fit rather neatly with the types of sacrifice. There are groves to hang victims, wells and mires to drown them, cliffs to hurl them from and stones to break them on. Perhaps, Adam of Bremen was not too wide of the mark when he suggested that the holiness of the trees at Uppsala was derived from the 'death and decay' of the victims which hung from them.

GENUINELY LOCAL CULTS

Although the great gods are often associated with trees, groves and wells, this does not mean that there were no cults which were absolutely local to a given site and its particular spirits. Such local cults might also focus on an earth-fast stone or a spring well, but without any association with a major universal god. Interestingly, while the Anglo-Saxon Ælfric writes of offerings at trees, stones and wells (*De falsis diis*), his Icelandic translator refers specifically to offerings for the land spirits, which are left by foolish women at flat stones (*Hauksbók*).

These land spirits also appear in *Landnámabók* and *Ulfljótslög*, and when Egil raises his scorn post he speaks of 'the land spirits that live in this land', though he also mentions a 'Land God' and 'Land Elf' who are probably more universal in nature (*Egils saga*, ch.56, 57). In the Icelandic *Kristni saga*, we meet Kodran, who lives at Gili River:

> At Gili River, stood a stone where he and his family had sacrificed, and said that their steward [*ár-maðr*, literally 'harvest-' or 'bounty-man'] lived in it.
>
> *Kristni saga*, ch.4

Interesting, if unreliable, details are added in the saga tale *Þorvalds þáttr ens víðförla*, where the 'steward' is called a 'prophet' (*spá-maðr*), and Kodran says that he can tell the future and also give sound practical advice (ch.2). A similar figure is associated with Goat-Björn in *Landnámabók*. Through such localised land spirits, people seem to have formed a spiritual bond with their home and homeland.

Even where there is a clear association between a cult site and a named god, the cult of the god might have taken over from an earlier, more localised, animistic cult. A likely example is found at the royal site of Jelling in Denmark. Here, set precisely midway between two large Viking-era burial mounds, is a massive boulder carved with a scene of the crucifixion. The precision with which the boulder is placed between the exact centres of the mounds arouses the suspicion that the boulder was here long before it was carved, and was in fact part of the original pre-Christian layout of the site. This suspicion seems to be confirmed by the discovery that the boulder rests on the original ground surface, whilst other layers have been built up around it. The Jelling boulder, which is a glacial erratic, is apparently an example of the sort of earth-fast stone which could form a focus for pre-Christian worship.

In fact, the religious connections of Jelling stretch back into the Bronze Age; the north mound incorporates an earlier Bronze-age mound, while two rows of standing stones from a very large monument, spread out on either side of the line between the two mounds. Unlike the sacred trees at Frösö and Gaesmere, the sacred stone at Jelling could not be felled and so it has been Christianised by carving. At Jelling, a Bronze-age cult place was clearly given a makeover by a Viking king in the name of some-or-other Viking god, and at a later date, a Christian king did the same again in the name of his own god.

Some writers have speculated that the cults of the great gods were typically aristocratic, whilst the common people would have worshipped local animistic spirits. However, although kings and nobles are inevitably associated with the most important temples, dedicated to the most important gods, there is no more evidence that kings ignored minor spirits than there is that peasants ignored the great gods. The poet of *Hárbarðsljóð* was aware of a social distinction in worship which, if somewhat exaggerated, seems to be borne out by other evidence. In this poem, which was probably composed in pre-Christian Norway, Odin claims not that the common people worshipped local spirits, but simply that they favoured a different god:

> Odin has earls who fall in battle,
> But Thor has the kindred of slaves.
>
> *Hárbarðsljóð*, st.24

STONES AND PILLARS

As at Jelling, large natural boulders could be a focus of worship. Another striking example of a pre-Christian earth-fast stone is Helligkvinde, or 'Holy Woman' on the Danish island of Bornholm. She is one of two standing stones on a ruined cairn beside the coastal road to Gudhjem ('God-home') and until recently, all travellers would bow to her. A nearby stone enclosure is known as 'Holy Woman's Children'. It is not possible to know whether the Holy Woman once stood for a particular named goddess. In Gudhjem itself, another pair of standing stones is known as Hestestenene, or 'The Horse's Stones', a name which seems the more resonant in light of the common choice of a horse as the sacrificial animal.

Phallic stones, roughly 8in to 20in high (20-50cm), are sometimes found at field edges in western Norway. More than 50 have been identified, dating probably from the third to eighth centuries. They are carved in pale stone, and are known today as 'holy white stones' (*hellige hvide stene*). A curious stone structure called Rögubben, or 'The Red Chap', stands on land belonging to a farm in Östergötland, Sweden, which has been called Rösten, or 'Red Stone', since at least the fourteenth century (*19*). The stone is regularly painted, and local tradition suggests it was once used as the focus of a fertility cult.

19 Rögubben 'The Red Chap' at Grebö (Östergötland, Sweden) is first recorded in the fourteenth century. He has a black-painted head, a white collar and a red body

Wood pillars as well as stone were the focus of ritual activity. The most famous sacred pillar was the Saxon 'Irminsul' at Eresburg, destroyed by Charles the Great in AD 772. Its importance is clear from the weight given to its destruction in all the Frankish annals. This Irminsul is said to have been part of a larger sacred site, including a holy grove and temple, with treasures of gold and silver. The pillar itself is described in a contemporary account in terms which recall the mythical Yggdrasil, upholding the nine worlds in its branches:

> They worshipped a wooden trunk of no small size, raised aloft beneath the heavens, called 'Irminsul' in their language, which means 'universal pillar', as it were 'the mainstay of everything'.
>
> *Translatio S. Alexandri*, ch.3

This translation for the word Irminsul is challenged by Widukind, who tells us that the Saxons worshipped Mars under the name 'Hermin', and that they set up a pillar to him to mark their victory over the Thuringians (*Res gestae saxonicae*). Probably, the Saxon word *irmin* was also used as an epithet of their god, just as its Norse cogate *jörmunr* (meaning 'vast') is listed among the names of Odin.

The Irminsul at Eresburg was not unique. One surviving example of a similar pillar was found in the sacred bog at Oberdorla in Thuringia; the bog contained more elaborate idols in various offering places, but at a height of 20ft (6m) the stark wooden pillar must have dominated the entire sanctuary. At the Anglo-Saxon palace of Yeavering, a curious narrow wooden 'amphitheatre' seems to have been focused on a single pillar.

Possible cousins of the Germanic earth-fast stones and sacred pillars are the classically-modelled 'Jupiter pillars' (*Jupitersäulen*) of Roman Germania. These stone columns usually stand about 12ft tall (4m), though a pillar from Mainz reaches 30ft (9m), and are crowned with an image of Jupiter. In Germania Superior, this is generally a mounted figure riding down a giant, whilst in Germania Inferior, an enthroned Jupiter is more common. Some later wooden columns might have been devoted Jupiter's local equivalent, the Germanic thunder god, but it would be unwise to assume that this was always the case.

IDOLS

In his *Germania*, Tacitus clearly states that the Germans do not 'liken [the gods] to any human appearance' (ch.9). Yet he seemingly contradicts himself when he comments that 'they carry into battle certain effigies and symbols taken from the holy groves' (*Germania*, ch.7). Possibly, he is referring to practices among different nations, or it might be that he has in mind effigies in non-human likeness. More probably, he means that whilst effigies might be made to represent a generalised human form, they are unlike the specific and realistic features of Greek and Roman art. When the fifth-century historian Sozomenos writes of a Gothic idol he calls the image a *xoanon*, a term which distinguishes the earliest unhewn or barely-worked idols from the elaborately carved sculptures of Classical religion. At any rate, there is solid evidence for Germanic idols from archaeology, from which it is also abundantly clear that delicate carving was quite inessential to their holiness.

Surviving idols come mostly from bogs, where the waterlogged peat has preserved the wood they are made from. Sometimes simple tall posts stood as idols surrounded by offerings, but at other times they were roughly carved into human form (*20*). Two of the most impressive are from Braak near Hamburg in Germany, where a 10ft male with erect phallus was accompanied by a slightly smaller female figure with similarly obvious sexual organs. Some such idols might once have stood on or near a cairn, as at Broddenbjerg in Denmark, and they are commonly surrounded by offerings, usually including pottery and animal bones, and sometimes with tools, wheels, flax and evidence of human sacrifice . A female figure from Ræbild, Denmark, was found with associated textiles which had probably clothed her, while clothing for idols is apparently alluded to in *Hávamál*:

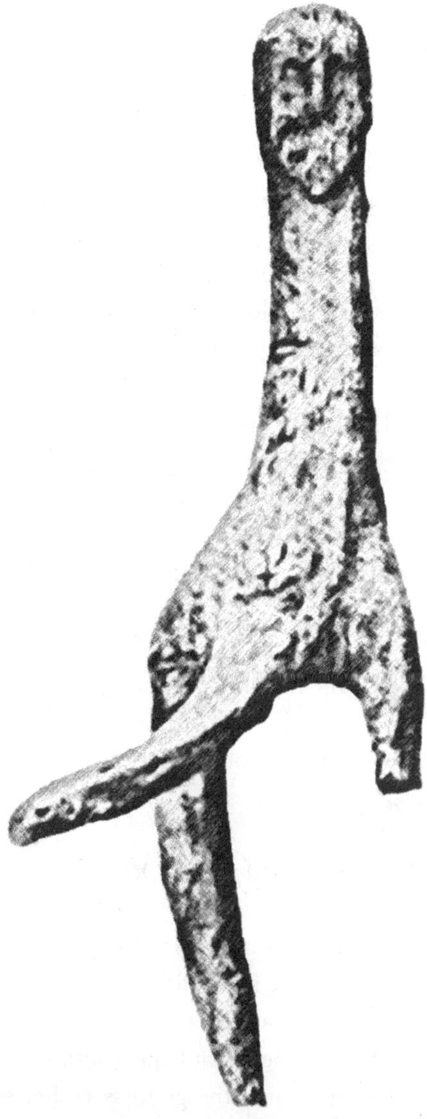

20 Phallic idol from Broddenbjerg, (Jylland, Denmark). The idol is about 40in tall (100cm) and was set on a cairn in the middle of a bog, surrounded by offerings. Minimal carving has been used to reveal the wood's natural affinity with the fertility god

> I gave my clothing on the plain
> to two wooden men;
> wearing linen they were important;
> naked, a man is ashamed.
>
> *Hávamál*, st.49

Similar outdoor shrines with idols are referred to in the historical record. Thus, Coifi's temple in Bede's *Historia Ecclesiastica* is a described as 'a place of idols' (Bk 2 ch.13). Ibn Fadlan describes how a Rus merchant takes his offerings before 'a tall upright wooden post with a face like a man's', which is surrounded by smaller idols representing 'the wives, daughters and sons of our Lord'. These shrines probably appeared very like those excavated by archaeologists in Germany and Denmark.

These carved figures doubtless represented named gods, but without very distinctive attributes, assigning a particular name to any individual idol is beyond the bounds of modern scholarship. However the phallic figures probably represent the fertility god Frey or his southern Germanic equivalent, while the pair of idols from Braak might indicate a shrine shared with his sister-consort Freyja.

WAGON IDOLS

It was believed of the goddess Nerthus that she travelled among men in her veiled wagon:

> On an island in the Ocean there is a sacred grove, where there is a holy vehicle covered in a cloth, which only the priest may touch. He knows when the goddess is within, and attends her with great reverence as female cattle draw her along. Then there is a holiday, a regional festival wherever she deigns to come and stay. They will not go to war; they will not take up arms; all iron is shut away; only then are peace and quiet known, only then are they cherished, until the same priest returns the goddess to her temple, when she has had enough of mortal companionship.
>
> *Germania*, ch.40

A similar tradition surrounds the god Lytir in the short saga story *Hauks þáttr hábrókar*, where the Swedish king Eirik consults Lytir – leading his wagon to a certain place and waiting until it grows heavy indicating the presence of the god, the wagon is then drawn to the king's hall, where Eirik greets Lytir, drinks a horn to him and asks him questions. In another brief saga story, *Gunnars þáttr helmings*,

Frey is also carried about the countryside in a wagon, but here it is clear that the god is in the shape of a wooden idol, a 'carved god'.

The Church historian Sozomenos tells how under the orders of Athanaric, a wooden image was drawn about in a wagon and worshipped by the Goths (*Historiae*, Bk 7 ch.37). 'An idol which they carry through the fields' mentioned in the *Indiculus Superstitionum et Paganiarum*, is reminiscent of the celebration of the Gallic goddess Berecynthia at Autun, whose image was borne around the new-sown fields in a wagon covered in a white veil, with singing and dancing (Gregory of Tours, *Liber in Gloria Confessorum*).

The wagon from the Oseberg ship burial, lavishly decorated and unmanœuvrable as it is, might suggest the sort of wagon which would have been used to carry such an idol. Similar wagons are shown with covered loads in a tapestry from the same burial, illustrating what might be a ritual procession. As well as the ship and wagon, the Oseberg burial included sledges, suggesting that vehicles might have held a special significance for the mound's occupant, who might have been a royal priestess (see below p.117). Finds of wheels and other wagon parts at sacred sites (as at Oberdorla and Rappendam) might also reflect the vehicles used to transport these gods. Two very fine wagons dating to the Roman Iron Age were excavated in the 1870s in the bog at Dejbjerg in Denmark (*21*). Each wagon was delicately made and was decorated with bronze plates. Such fine vehicles might well have been used in ritual processions.

21 One of two Iron-age wagons from Dejbjerg (Jylland, Denmark), which might once have drawn an idol like that of the goddess Nerthus. The wagons had been deliberately deposited in the bog

When a wagon idol is identifiable as a god or goddess in the Germanic pantheon, it is always from the group of fertility deities known in Scandinavian sources as the Vanir, who were distinguished from the principal tribe of gods, the Æsir. Frey and Nerthus are certainly Vanir deities, and the association with fields is within the sphere of the Vanir gods. Lytir was presumably another Vanir deity, or alternatively might have been identical with Frey.

One of the most curious features of these wagon idols is that they are hidden. Whereas other idols were made to be clearly visible, these idols may not be seen by ordinary worshippers. Instead, each is tended by a single priest or priestess who seems to be seen as the spouse of the god. According to Tacitus, when according to custom, other attendants are required to bathe the goddess Nerthus, they are afterwards killed, just as Actaeon is killed after he sights the bathing Artemis.

EPHEMERAL IDOLS

Many of the provisions of *Indiculus Superstitionum et Paganiarum* have a decidedly homely ring to them. Provisions 26 and 27 concern idols of flour and idols of cloth. The medieval Norwegian Eidsivathing's Law prohibits idols made of dough or clay, while in *Friðþjófs saga*, the women sit by the fire baking 'gods' (ch.4). Bede gives the name *sol monath* for February, calling it 'the month of the cakes which, in it, they used to offer to their gods'. The Anglo-Saxon 'Land Remedy' also calls for a specially baked cake or loaf, which is sacrificed by placing it under the first furrow.

Gingerbread men are still associated with Christmas in England, and small spiced cakes shaped in various images are eaten at festivals in Germany and Scandinavia. Some of these cakes are strongly reminiscent of images on gold foils from Vendel and Viking sites in

22 A *guldgubbe* from Bornholm. These *guldgubber* or 'gold chaps' are made from tiny pieces of gold foil weighing only a couple of grains (*c*.0.1g)

Scandinavia. Large numbers of these foils, known as *guldgubber* have been found at cult centres, in buildings and at field edges (*22*). Their function is unknown, but they might possibly have been associated with baked idols. If not, their use might nonetheless have been analogous.

PERSONAL IDOLS AND AMULETS

As well as large idols linked with a specific place of worship and idols drawn about in cult wagons, there seem to have been miniature portable idols. Thus, *Vatnsdæla saga*, *Landnámabók* and *Ynglinga saga* all tell the story of a pocket Frey which King Harald Hairfair gave to Ingimund and which emigrated to Iceland before him. Somewhat more credibly, in *Hallfreðar saga Vandræðaskálds* (ch.6) Kalf betrays Hallfred's continuing fondness for the old gods, telling the king that 'in his pouch he has a likeness of Thor made from a walrus tusk'.

A little figure made in walrus ivory from Lund in southern Sweden has been interpreted as the god Thor (*23*). He is seated in a chair and clutches his beard with both hands. Another walrus-ivory figure from Baldursheimur in Iceland sits cross-legged clutching his beard with both hands. Similar figures made in amber and bronze have been found at Feddet in Denmark, Chernaia Mogila in Ukraine and Eyrarland in Iceland (*24* & *25*). Many of these have been identified individually as images of Thor and most recently Richard Perkins has argued that all these beard-clutching figures represent the god Thor blowing into his beard to raise a wind.

Not all pocket idols represent Thor. A cross-legged bronze image from Rällinge in Sweden, with erect phallus, clutching his beard with one hand, the other resting on his knee, probably represents Frey, while a standing figure in bronze from Lindby in southern Sweden with only one eye represents Odin (*26* & *27*). All these images stand between 1½in and 2¾in high (4-7cm).

23 Whalebone figure from Lund (Skåne, Sweden), probably representing the god Thor. Height: 1⅞in (4.7cm)

Above left: 24 Bronze figure from Chernaia Mogila (Chernigov, Ukraine), probably representing the god Thor. Height: 1¾in (4.6cm)

Above right: 25 Bronze figure from Akureyri in Eyrarland, Iceland, probably representing the god Thor. Height: 2⅝in (6.7cm)

Left: 26 Bronze figure from Rällinge (Södermanland, Sweden), probably representing the god Frey. Height: 2¾in (6.9cm)

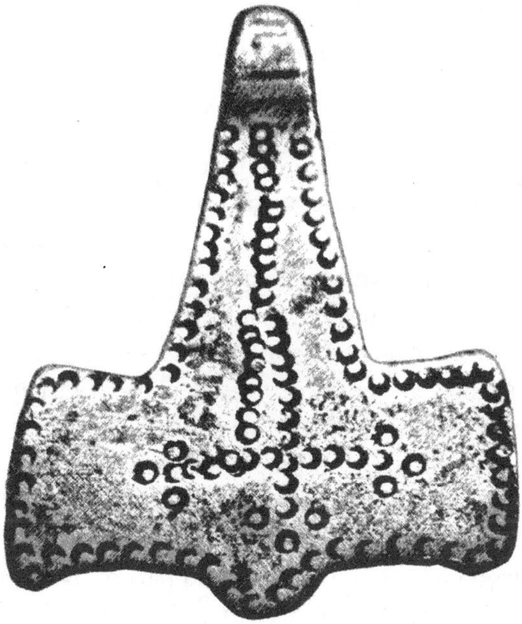

Above left: 27 Bronze figure from Lindby (Skåne, Sweden), probably representing the god Odin. Height: 2¾in (6.9cm)

Above right: 28 Thor's Hammer from Fønsskov (Fyn, Denmark), now in the National Museum of Denmark

Right: 29 Hammer amulet from Ash (Kent, England). There seems every reason to believe that early Jutish hammer amulets are the precursors of the later Scandinavian Thor's Hammers

The most famous of all pre-Christian amulets is Thor's hammer (*28*). At the Viking town of Birka, excavation of 1100 graves has yielded 27 Thor's hammer pendants. Most of these are from the tenth century, and it has been suggested that the hammer was adopted in response to the Christian cross. However, the earlier use of hammer amulets is attested by the burial of a Viking at Repton in England, who probably died at the time of the Great Army's occupation in AD 873-4. Thor's hammer rings appear in the Mälar region of Sweden in the eighth century, and the earliest known Danish example comes from a woman's cremation urn from Nebel (now in northern Germany) dated to *c.*800. Jutish examples from Ash and Gilton in Anglo-Saxon Kent date to the sixth century (*29*). Like pocket idols, these amulets are portable objects expressing personal devotion, but unlike the idols, they were probably worn conspicuously.

An altogether different kind of amulet is sometimes found in the graves of early Anglo-Saxon women, who were often buried with a single small, round, ancient object, carried in a purse. These objects would presumably have been owned by the women in their lifetimes, and part of their significance must lie in their age, which may have associated them with remote ancestors or local spirits.

In her study of Anglo-Saxon amulets, Audrey Meaney notes that, in general, Anglo-Saxon men do not seem to have worn amulets as such. In Denmark too, amulets are almost exclusively associated with women. In Sweden and Norway, amulets also occur most often in women's graves, but they are sometimes found in men's graves. Thus, whilst in Denmark all Thor's hammers found in graves come from women's graves, in Sweden by contrast, 40 per cent are from men's graves.

To some extent, men had their own amulet-like objects. In the Vendel period, men wore helmets decorated with boar-crests, which probably had a protective significance (*30*), and runes adorning swords must also have been imbued with magical power. Warriors also appear to have developed strong attachments to their weapons, and these might have fulfilled some of the roles of personal amulets.

Although the legend of Ingimund's Frey is set in the earlier Viking period, the surviving pocket images along with most of the Thor's hammers date from the close of the pre-Christian era in Scandinavia. These are objects of personal devotion and might indicate a new personalised relationship with the gods, perhaps with the pocket images indicating that individuals might want to express their personal piety in secret, as in the case of Hallfred. Hammer pendants by contrast suggest deliberate conspicuous display of religious identity.

Not all amulets were used for personal piety and Price draws attention to the deliberate burial of amulets in road building at Birka. Perhaps amulets could also be used as small sacrificial offerings, like *guldgubber*.

DECORATED IDOLS

> Thor sat in the middle. He was the most honoured. He was huge, and all arrayed in gold and silver. Thor was fitted out so that he sat in a chariot. This was very magnificent; two wooden goats were harnessed in front of it, very finely worked. It all ran on wheels, both the chariot and the goats. There were ropes of twisted silver on the goats horns, and everything was made with very skilful craftsmanship.
>
> *Flateyjarbók, Ólafs saga Tryggvasonar*

Not without reason perhaps, it has been doubted whether this description of Thor's idol at Mære in Norway is entirely accurate, but the notion of such an elaborate idol should not be dismissed out of hand. The prestige of the temple could be a source of pride for local chieftains. Such a centrepiece would certainly add to their renown and might well have been perceived by the temple patron as a gift in honour of the god. Even if this account exaggerates the splendour of such an object, it is probably based on a tradition that a very fine idol had once existed at Mære. Though this is the most elaborate, it is not the only description of a lavishly decorated idol. Not all idols, it seems, were simple wooden *xoanoi*.

Left: 30 Boarhelms on warriors from a helmet plaque. The boar crest on the helmet seems to have been an amulet of sorts

Right: 31 Carefully worked wooden idol from Rude Eskildstrup (Sjælland, Denmark). This idol has been dated to the sixth century and wears a triple neck ring

In Snorri's version of *Ólafs saga Tryggvasonar*, Thor's idol at Mære is 'decked in gold and silver' (ch.69/76); there is no mention of any elaborate accessories, but Snorri's version is nearly always briefer than the 'biggest' (*mesta*) version of *Flateyjarbók*. In *Ólafs saga helga*, the son of the chieftain Dala-Gudbrand describes Thor's idol at Hundorp in Gudbrandsdalen, Norway:

> That evening, the king asked Gudbrand's son how their god was made. He said that he was modelled on Thor 'and he has a hammer in his hand, and he is very big and hollow inside, and beneath him is a platform which he stands on when he is outside. He lacks no gold nor silver on him. Four loaves of bread are brought to him every day, along with meat.'
>
> *Ólafs saga helga*, ch.112

Another image of Thor riding in a chariot is described in *Njáls saga* (ch.88). The saga says that this temple is at Dala-Gudbrand's home, so it ought to be the same figure that is described by Dala-Gudbrand's son, which is clearly not mounted in a chariot. However, the temple described in *Njáls saga*, which includes images of Hakon's personal deities Thorgerd and Irpa, is more likely to be Hakon's than Gudbrand's, if it ever existed at all, and indeed the saga itself seems to express doubt as to whose temple it is.

In the Icelandic *Heimlysing*, we read of idols made in human form out of 'red gold or white silver' as well as wood and stone; this detail does not seem to be one of the many which is copied from Isidore's *Etymologiae*. Adam describes the idols at Uppsala as seated in a temple 'completely furnished with gold', and it is likely that the idols were also golden.

Many of the wooden idols recovered by archaeologists are extremely crudely carved, but some, such as those from Rude Eskildstrup in Denmark, and Oberdorla and Possendorf in Germany, are artistically interesting and carefully worked (*31*). The little eleventh-century personal idols described above are also finely made, and might support accounts of larger beautifully worked idols in contemporary temples. Viking workmanship could be staggeringly elaborate. The animal head posts from the Oseberg burial might give some idea of just how richly decorated some images might have been.

However, whilst the idols described in the sagas are sometimes resplendent with gold and silver, it is only the *Flateyjarbók* description quoted above that includes elaborate decoration, and even here it seems that the finest workmanship was lavished on the idol's accoutrements, rather than on the god itself.

CHAPTER 4

TEMPLES, PRIESTS AND FESTIVALS

TEMPLES

Tacitus says that the gods of the Germans were not confined within walls (*Germania*, ch.9), and indeed the surviving wooden idols seem all to have come from open-air locations. The ancient moss-grown idol discovered by Ogmund the Dane on the island of Samsø must also have stood outside (*Ragnars saga loðbrókar*, ch.20). However temples containing idols appear repeatedly in medieval accounts. Frankish accounts are rarely specific, but give a general impression of temple buildings associated with idols. Bede records a letter in which Pope Gregory calls for idols to be removed from Anglo-Saxon temples, so that they can be reused as churches (*Historia Ecclesiastica*, Bk 1 ch.30).

Scandinavian sources such as *Landnámabók*, *Flateyjarbók*, *Njáls saga* and *Eyrbyggja saga* also describe idols housed in pre-Christian temples. Especially interesting, since as an incidental detail it serves as unwitting testimony, is the case of the idol of Thor at Mære in *Ólafs saga helga*, which had to be kept inside in wet weather, but is brought out at meetings when the weather allows (ch.112). Richly decorated idols are very likely to have been kept indoors out of the rain.

Probably the most famous account of a Scandinavian temple is Adam of Bremen's description of the temple at Uppsala in Sweden, which stood beside the sacred grove described above.

> This nation has a very famous temple called Uppsala, situated not far from the city of Sigtuna. In this temple, which is completely furnished in gold, the images of three gods are worshipped by the people. As the mightiest of them, Thor has his throne in the middle of the room; the places on either side of him are taken by Wodan and Fricco …
>
> *Gesta Hammaburgensis ecclesiae pontificum*, Bk 4 ch.26

A much later document claims that the stone church, which was completed in 1150, was built up against the temple, which was then still standing (though presumably converted for use as a church) and Sune Lindqvist believed that the shape of the temple was discernible on the church wall. More recently Else Nordahl has cast doubt on the very notion of a temple as such at Uppsala and prefers to see Adam's description as based upon vague hearsay combined with biblical sources.

Adam of Bremen's description of the temple at Uppsala forms part of a wider discussion of the Scandinavian peoples, but in his whole account he does not mention any temples other than that at Uppsala. Clearly, Adam felt that the temple at Uppsala was remarkable and this is why he incorporates it. In his opening sentence, he describes the temple as 'very famous' (*nobilissimus*) and he might well have expected his readers to know about it already. Interestingly, Adam places the idols in a 'dining room' (*triclinium*), a detail which is certainly not drawn from biblical accounts or from descriptions of Roman temples, and which suggests that he had specific knowledge of how the temple feast was arranged. Adam does not otherwise mention eating at all and his use of the word 'dining room' here suggests that, far from elaborating his account from meagre sources, he actually knew rather more than he tells. The idols in the 'dining room' at Uppsala corroborate Snorri's account of the sacrificial meal and toasts quoted before (p.25, *Hákonar saga Aðalsteinsfóstra*, ch.14). Together, these independent sources make a strong case for a Scandinavian tradition of indoor sacrificial feasts. This means that the pre-Christian temple would in effect have been a feasting hall.

Feasting halls are associated with royal sites such as Uppsala in both literature and archaeology. At Uppsala are the remains of two large halls, each built on a raised platform, and these great feasting halls might actually be identical with Adam's temple. At Huseby in Norway, a similar structure has recently been uncovered near the Viking trading port of Kaupang, which is thought to have been the ancient royal hall of Skíringssalr, where the Norwegian kings held sacrifices. The names Uppsala and Huseby both apparently refer to such temple halls, one meaning 'The High Hall' and the other 'The Settlement at the House'. As well as the Norse words '*salr*' and '*hus*' (Old English '*sele*' and '*hus*') such a building could also be called a 'hall' (Old Norse '*höll*', Old English '*heall*').

However, the Scandinavian temple hall seems particularly to have been described by the word *hof*. Within Scandinavia, the term *hof*, which in the wider Germanic world simply denotes a secular building or enclosure, comes to be associated with places of worship, and is commonly translated as 'temple'. Thus, in *Austrfaravísur*, the eleventh-century poet Sigvatr says he came to a farm called 'Hof', whose people said it was holy and that they were celebrating a religious festival inside. In Norway, there are over a hundred farms with names derived from the word *hof*.

32 A reconstruction of the great hall at Lejre (Sjælland, Denmark) which stood 158ft long by 36ft wide (48 x 11m). A hall like this would have been used as a hof, where the sacrificial meal was consumed and where idols might have been housed

As well as the hall buildings at Uppsala and Huseby, large halls have been found at kings' and chieftains' farms, and at known temple sites at Borg on Lofoten, Hofstaðir in Iceland, Högom in Sweden, Lejre in Denmark and Mære in Norway, among other places (*32*). Most recently, two large halls have been located at Borre in Norway, close to the well-known grave mounds. Similarly, at Jelling, Denmark, the remains of a possible hall have been uncovered in close proximity to the glacial erratic stone which might have been the original centre of worship at the site. The royal hall at Lejre was 160ft long (50m) and that at Uppsala was 200ft (60m), while the hall at Borg on Lofoten was a massive 280ft long (85m) and 50ft wide (15m).

Hákonar saga (in *Flateyjarbók* and *Codex Frisianus*) describes how King Hakon built feasting halls (*veizlu-höll*) at places called Hof and Husaby. *Ynglinga saga* tells how King Ingjald built a second hall at Uppsala 'no less magnificent than the High Hall (*Upp-salr*) was', which had thrones for six kings inside. No doubt one of the hall mounds at Uppsala is in fact the remains of Ingjald's hall of six kings. Likewise, in the Anglo-Saxon poem *Beowulf*, the Danish king Hrothgar decides to build a new feasting hall:

It came to his mind
That he would have a hall building,
A mighty mead-house made by men,
Greater than any that had ever been heard of.

Beowulf, lines 66b-9

The temple with its 'dining room' described by Adam might not have been dedicated solely to the worship of the gods, but doubled as the king's feasting hall.

Eyrbyggja saga contains a fascinating if questionable description of the inside of the hall or *hof* at Hofstaðir:

> He had a temple (*hof*) built there, and it was a big house. There was a door in the side wall near one end. Further in stood the holy pillars (*öndvegis-súlurnar*), and there were nails in them that are called 'god nails' (*regin-naglar*). Further in, everything was sanctuary (*friðar-staðr*). Inside the temple was a building rather like the choir in a church now, and there stood an altar (*stalli*) in the middle of the floor like a church altar, and on it there lay a ring without a join, weighing twenty ounces, on which all oaths were sworn. That ring had to be worn by the temple priest (*hof-goði*) at all public meetings. On the altar there had to be a *hlaut*-bowl with a *hlaut*-twig like a sprinkler … The gods were arranged around the altar in the chamber.
>
> *Eyrbyggja saga*, ch.4

This saga was written long after the introduction of Christianity and it seems the writer or his source has been rather too eager to provide familiar analogies. In particular, the references to churches give the false impression that the pre-Christian temple was analogous to a Christian church. However, some aspects of the description do seem to square with evidence from archaeology and other sources, and overall it seems likely that the *Eyrbyggja saga* account has some basis in authentic tradition. Certainly, when the saga goes on to say that it was the priest's responsibility to hold sacrificial feasts within the temple, this cannot have been influenced by analogies with Christian practice. *Eyrbyggja saga*'s description of a *hof* with idols and altar, where the sacrificial meal was eaten, is in essence very similar to Adam's account of idols set up in a 'dining room' or *triclinium.*

Recent scholarship emphasises the role of the *hof* as the hall of the local chieftain, which might be used for religious celebrations if necessary. However, as conceived by later medieval Icelanders, the *hof* also housed idols and other paraphernalia, and there seems little reason to doubt this tradition. Perhaps, we should simply shift our perspective, so that we see the *hof* not as a secular building with religious functions, but as a religious building with secular functions. The Icelandic word for a chieftain is *goði*, or 'priest', and by this reading, the pre-Christian chieftain, the leader of the community who organises the local legal assembly, does not simply go by the name of priest, his very house is in fact a religious sanctuary. From a modern perspective, the distinction between secular and religious institutions often seems to have been blurred in the pre-Christian world, and it is probably best not to try to pigeonhole the Scandinavian *hof* according to these terms.

In English place names, words for shrine and temple are linked with personal names rather than the names of gods. The word *weoh* occurs in Patchway near Brighton, which is 'the *weoh* of Pæccel', and in an estate called *Cusan weoh*, 'the *weoh* of Cusa' which once existed near Farnham. The word *hearg* can be associated with community names; thus Harrow in Middlesex first appears in a charter of the year 767 as 'the *hearg* of the people of Guma', and another charter refers to a lost '*hearg* of the people of Besa' which, like Cusa's *weoh* was located near Farnham. Thus, Anglo-Saxon shrines appear to have been named after their owners and the communities they served, and might have had secular as well as religious significance.

The temple at Köln in the Rhineland might have been set up as a feasting hall; in his *Vita S. Galli*, Gregory of Tours says that there 'the neighbouring barbarians used to make offerings and stuff themselves with food and drink' (*Vita Patriae*, ch.6.2).

TEMPLE BUILDINGS

Not all descriptions of temples can be dismissed as chieftains' halls. Thus, Bede records the comment of Pope Gregory, that 'the temples of idols should not be destroyed … for if these temples are well built, it is necessary that they are turned from the worship of devils to the service of the true God' (*Historia Ecclesiastica*, Bk 1, ch.30). He also tells how, in the early seventh century, Raedwald had a temple which doubled as a Christian church and which must have stood for at least 50 years (Bk 2 ch.15).

A curious building at the Anglo-Saxon royal site at Yeavering was associated with a large stockpile of ox skulls presumably from sacrifices. One of the unusual features of the building itself was a line of three postholes inside the house, which cannot have served any structural purpose and which might have supported an altar or images of the gods. This is perhaps the sort of 'well-built temple' which Pope Gregory had in mind, and although the kingdom of Northumbria was only converted after Gregory's death, this building was transformed into a church as his letter had decreed.

The most important archaeological evidence for a 'well-built temple' in Scandinavia comes from Uppåkra in Skåne, Sweden. Here, in 2001, in a flat field to the south of the modern church, archaeologists began to uncover the site of an Iron-age building, which has been interpreted as 'a temple of the Æsir'. Some time in the Roman era, probably around the year 200, a strong stave-built house was erected on the site of an earlier long house. Over the next 500 years, this unusual house was rebuilt several times, each structure being almost identical with the preceding one. It is thought to have been a tall and impressive building, similar to a medieval stave church but with a central hearth. Perhaps it was a building such as this that the poet of *Grímnismál* had in mind, when he described Njörd's hall as a 'high-timbered temple' (*hörgr*, st.16).

At the western end of the Uppåkra temple, there were two doorways, standing opposite each other in the north and south walls; there was also a third doorway in the south-east. The south-western door was probably the main entrance, marked with a prominent porch, while the area around the north-western doorway was marked with a large number of buried finds, particularly the little gold foils known as *guldgubber*. Similar gold foils are also associated with *hof* sites at Mære and Borg.

Other places where a building has been interpreted as a dedicated temple, as opposed to a chieftain's *hof*, include Sanda, Borg and Järrestad in Sweden, and Tissø in Denmark. However, whether these are genuinely temple sites or not, it is possible that worship was focused outside rather than within the temple walls.

At Uppåkra, for instance, although a glass bowl and decorative bronze beaker had been deposited inside the building as well as many *guldgubber*, most of the finds suggesting sacrifice were in the area surrounding the temple, where a great number of spearheads have been found. Many of these spearheads had been deliberately bent or 'killed'. Other war gear had also been sacrificed here, including slingshot, arrows and shields, and some of these too had been ritually 'killed' before they were deposited. There were artfully made helmet mounts, and lavishly inlaid and gilded sword fittings. There were also human bones, but no complete skeletons. The whole scene is reminiscent of the descriptions of sacred hoards described by Caesar, Tacitus and Orosius (see above, p.27).

A rather different kind of temple building is alluded to in the law of the Norwegian Gulathing, which states that one may not make a house and call it a shrine (*hörgr*). The *Indiculus Superstitionum et Paganiarum* contains a clause 'Of the little houses, that is sanctuaries.' It seems reasonable to suppose that these 'little houses' are too small to live in, perhaps even too small to enter, and this might well be the sort of 'house' that the Gulathing law refers to. Thus, it is the house itself which appears to be the focus of worship, and there is no indication that it need contain religious images, any more than they are needful at a holy grove or well. On the island of Gotland, two distinct forms of stone monument are commonly found together, which Andrén believes represent the doors and hearth of a house. These symbolic 'houses' are usually set on the border between cultivated land and 'wild' land such as woods. Remains of fires and animal bones found around the stones suggest they might have been used for religious rites and ritual meals.

While the *hof* was in essence a practical addition to a place of worship rather than an inherently holy structure, the *hörgr* seems to have been built as a focus for worship in itself. Both *hof* and *hörgr* can be described as 'temples', and we should be aware that this word can cover buildings with significantly different functions. The word *hörgr* might be derived from an ancient term for a holy place. It appears in Old English as *hearg* and in Old High German as *harug*, with a range of meanings encompassing 'altar', 'holy grove', 'sanctuary', 'place of worship' and 'idol', as well as non-religious meanings of 'woodland', 'cairn' and 'mountain'.

The *hörgr* could take various forms. In the cases mentioned above, it seems to have been a house; sometimes it was probably merely symbolic, being unusually small or even lacking walls. At other times, a *hörgr* might have taken the form of a cairn, but again the idea might have been that it would provide a dwelling-place for the god. The Anglo-Saxon *hearg* is thought to have involved a cairn, since *hearg* place names are associated with hilltops, as at Harrow-on-the-Hill, Middlesex. At Broddenbjerg in Denmark, a phallic wooden idol was set on a cairn in a bog, surrounded by offerings, and in the poem *Hyndluljóð*, the goddess Freyja says of her protégé Ottar:

> A *hörgr* he built me, stacked with stones
> (now that gravel has turned into glass)
> reddened anew with ox's blood;
> Ottar would always trust in goddesses.
>
> *Hyndluljóð*, st.10

Possibly similar in intent are the enclosures associated with sacred sites, which might have separated sacred space from the ordinary world.

ENCLOSURES AND BOUNDARIES

> If anyone should make a vow at trees, or at wells, or at stones, or else at fences … this is sacrilege, that is worship of demons.
>
> *Liber Pœnitentialis*

The trees, wells and stones of this eighth-century Anglo-Latin text are, by now, the familiar hallmarks of pre-Chistian holy places – but what of the fences?

The thirteenth-century Gotland law (*Guta lag*) contains a provision against a *staf-garðr* (literally 'pole-yard' or 'pole-fence') meaning 'sanctuary'. The term, which is also used in *Guta saga* (ch.1), suggests an enclosed space, apparently surrounded by wooden posts. Bede twice mentions the fenced enclosures (*septa*) at King Edwin's Northumbrian temple at Goodmanham (*Historia Ecclesiatica* Bk 2 ch.13) so when the *Laws of the Northumbrian Priests* speak of 'a sanctuary round a stone or tree or well', we may imagine that this sanctuary was defined by a similar boundary.

In bog deposits at Thorsbjerg and at Vimose, a small area was enclosed by a wattle fence, and it was within this fence that the main deposits were laid. At Oberdorla, the edge of the holy pool was partly surrounded by timber and wattle fences. Likewise, at Trelleborg, sacrificial wells were associated with small enclosures surrounded by low dykes.

Some vague literary references to temples might not indicate anything more than fences and dykes of the sort found at Oberdorla and Trelleborg, or suggested by Bede's description of Goodmanham. Thus, for instance, in the *Vita Sturmi*, when Charles the Great urges the Saxons to 'forsake idols and images … destroy the temples of the gods, cut down the groves …', there is no clear reason to think that he has anything in mind beyond the sorts of fenced enclosures which we know from archaeology. However, the structures referred to as 'pole-yards' and fences could sometimes have been even less substantial. At Norwegian gatherings, the place where the legal committee (*lög-rétta*) sat was surrounded by ropes called 'sanctuary bands' (*vé-bönd*) which were borne on wooden poles (*Egils saga*, ch.56; *Hundabrævið*; *Frostaþings lag*). The importance of these boundary markers in defining the sanctuary is clear in *Egils saga* (ch.56) and in the *Vita Lebuini*, where people cut the ropes and tear down the poles which hold them, to break up the sanctuary and begin a fight. In both these accounts the areas are hallowed for the practice of law and so are sanctuaries of peace, but earlier in *Egils saga*, a similar cordon surrounds a battlefield (ch.52).

Such bands or boundaries appear to have marked out the limits of the sacred space. In defining the limits of the sacred, these boundaries take on a sacred purpose in themselves, and this might be one reason why the gods themselves are referred to as 'bands' or 'bonds' (*bönd*), and the temples are 'the sanctuaries of the bands' (*vé banda*, *Vellekla* st.15).

We have already referred repeatedly to Adam of Bremen's description of the temple at Uppsala. In this context, it is a later addition which adds the most interesting detail:

> A gold chain surrounds that temple, hanging over the gables of the hall, and it glitters from afar as people approach.
>
> *Gesta Hammaburgensis ecclesiae pontificum*, Bk 4 ch.26 Schol.135

Many scholars have cast doubt on this golden chain at Uppsala, but it would seem to be simply a more elaborate version of the 'sanctuary bands' (*vé-bönd*) which marked out other sanctuaries. These 'bands' appear to have defined the sanctuary within them, and the sanctuary was broken when they were removed. Perhaps, the hall at Uppsala was only sacred because of its golden chain. It could even be that it is the band which transforms the feasting hall (*hof*) into a sanctuary (*vé*).

PRIESTS

Adam's account also tells us that the temple at Uppsala was tended by priests, who offered sacrifice on behalf of the nation (*Gesta Hammaburgensis*, Bk 4 ch.27).

It is likely that, throughout the period, people conducted their own private religious observances. Thus, al-Turtushi describes seeing the carcasses of victims outside people's houses, Ibn Fadlan describes merchants conducting their own sacrifices at a public temple, and in *Egils saga*, Egil sacrifices a horse to raise his scorn post, and a bull for his duel (ch.57, 66). Tacitus also describes religious ceremonies conducted by the head of the household:

> Then, the priest of the community if it is a public consultation, or the head of the household if private, looks up to heaven and prays to the gods …
>
> *Germania*, ch.10

Just as private consultations are conducted by the 'head of the household' (*pater familiae*), so the 'priest of the community' (*sacerdos civitatis*) might also have wielded secular authority within the community as a political leader or landowner. Elsewhere, Tacitus reveals that the ancient Germanic priests had legal powers similar to those of later Scandinavian chieftains (*Germania*, ch.7, 11).

In medieval Iceland, even after the introduction of Christianity, the secular chieftain went by the title of 'priest' (*goði*). Similarly, an eighth-century German glossary renders the Latin word *tribunus*, 'tribune, magistrate', with Old High German *cotinc* (*Codex Abrogans* 75). The German word is clearly from the same root as the Scandinavian *goði*, and shows the same association of priestly and secular power. English shrines seem to have generally been named after individual landowners, suggesting a similar system of chieftain-priests might have operated in pre-Christian Anglo-Saxon England.

Writing in the eleventh-century, Archbishop Wulfstan of York distinguishes between the priests of the pagan gods whom he calls *þenas* or 'thanes', and priests of the Christian God whom he calls *þeowas* or 'slaves' (*Sermo Lupi*). Both words have the meaning of 'servant', but whereas the word chosen for the servants of the heathen gods suggests noblemen serving their king, the word he chooses for Christian servants denotes slavery. The priests of the Viking Danelaw were apparently well-to-do landlords, akin to the Icelandic *goðar*. The same word is used of a priest and chieftain on an early ninth-century runestone from Glavendrup on the Danish island of Fyn, which memorialises 'Alli the Pale, priest (**kuþi**; *goði*) of the sanctuary, the host's noble thane'.

The role of the 'priest' is thus an extension of the role of the head of the household. Just as the individual household looks to the *pater familiae* for leadership, so the people of a region look to their chieftain. There is thus a clear continuity between secular power and leadership in religious ceremonies, but the religious role of the chieftains does not seem to entail religious authority as such. It was the chieftain's responsibility to organise both the legal and the religious affairs of his community. Since the main religious rite was sacrifice and a shared meal, the chieftain is the patron of the feast; the role of the 'headman' (*höfðingi*) at such a feast is described in *Hákonar saga Aðalsteinsfóstra* (ch.14, quoted above p.25). There is no evidence that the priest or chieftain had any divine mandate or sanction. As a priest, he represents his people to his gods; he does not represent his gods to his people.

According to the later Irish medieval account *Cogadh Gaedhel re Gallaibh*, when the Viking war-leader Turgeis conquered Armagh, he 'usurped the abbacy', setting himself up as the new priest. Turgeis expects his Irish subjects to accept his religious leadership as a corollary of his secular leadership. *Cogadh Gaedhel* sees this as a deliberate attempt to supplant Christianity in Ireland, but in reality it is probably only from a Christian perspective that Turgeis appears to be at war with Christianity; he himself is simply fulfilling his proper role as chieftain. In this way, a relatively small number of high-status settlers might transform the religious environment of their new home.

TEMPLE TOLLS

> Everyone had to pay toll (*tollr*) to the temple and should be with the temple priest on all journeys, just like thing-men now with their chieftains, but the priest had to maintain it at his own expense so that it didn't decay, and to have sacrificial feasts in it.
>
> *Eyrbyggja saga*, ch.4

The same system is described in *Hauksbók*, and *Vápnfirðinga saga* (ch.5). In *Kristni saga*, some Christian Icelanders refuse to pay the temple toll. Chieftains received dues from their followers, which, theoretically at least, went towards the upkeep of the temple and sacrifice. *Ynglinga saga* also notes that in return for these taxes, the chieftain had to defend the country from enemies (ch.8).

The English Archbishop Wulfstan apparently refers to the temple toll, writing that 'among heathen peoples, they dare not withhold little or much of that which is allotted to the honour of false gods, and everywhere we withhold God's tithes all too often' (*Sermo Lupi*). Although some writers have doubted the truth of later Icelandic accounts, Wulfstan was writing about contemporary practices amongst Scandinavians in England. Public subscription to the temple seems to go back to even earlier times, since Tacitus notes that animals were kept at public expense in the sacred woods and groves (*Germania*, ch.10). The wealth of temples as described by Caesar or despoiled by Charlemagne, is probably largely the product of this system of tolls.

Tolls paid to temples represent the individual householder's share in the communal sacrifice. Thus, the communal religious sacrifice is not just the favour of the chieftain, but the right of the free man. The temple ring, which was legally required in every temple and on which the 'law oath' was sworn, might have symbolised the extended wealth of the temple in the ongoing sacrificial offering of dues by the community as a whole. As such, it would have been a highly appropriate object on which to take an oath, representing everyone's equal commitment and contribution to the sacrifice.

As well as the regular temple toll, fines imposed in legal suits might also have gone towards the upkeep of the temple. A runic ring associated with the assembly site at Hög in Sweden, sheds some light on the payment of fines to the temple. This iron ring, which now hangs in the church at Forsa, is 17in across (43cm) and is inscribed with nearly 250 runes (*33*). Although it has long been (somewhat oddly) dated to the Christian period, the apparent reasons for a late date have now been dismissed, and it can take its rightful place as an important artefact of the Viking Age; Brink has dubbed it 'The oldest law of the North'. The inscription reads:

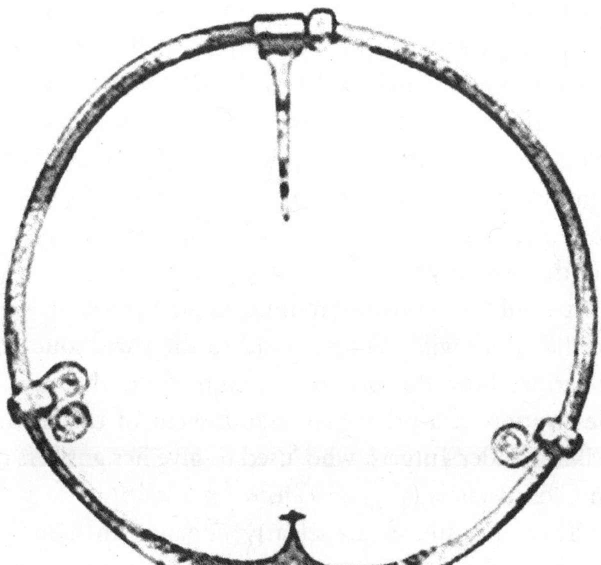

33 This iron ring, which now hangs in the church at Forsa is believed to have come from neighbouring Hög (Hälsingland, Sweden). Its terse runic inscription concerns payments for the upkeep of the pre-Christian temple.

> An ox to the temple's taxes (**at uis kilan**; *at vés gildjum*), and two pennies a staff for the first time;
> Two oxen and four pennies for the next time;
> But for the third time, four oxen and eight pennies a staff, and all possessions impounded, if he has not made amends.
> This the nation has in national law, as was decreed before and hallowed.
> And they themselves made this, Anund from Tåsta and Ofeig from Hjortsta. And Vibjörn wrote.

Albeit that the exact context of these fines is unclear, there is no question that the moneys raised go towards the community's temple, and the 'temple's taxes' or 'funds' of the Forsa Ring match the payment of a toll in *Eyrbyggja saga* and elsewhere.

PRIESTESSES

The Icelandic word *gyðja*, 'priestess', represents the female form of *goði*, 'priest'. Sometimes, a *gyðja* seems to be in charge of a temple or chieftaincy, as in *Vápnfirðinga saga* (ch.5), where we meet Steinvör who 'was temple priestess there, and administered the main temple', or *Landnámabók*, where we read of the priestess Thurid, who married Thorstein. However, these female chieftains are a rarity and at other times the word appears to be used to mean the wife of the priest (*goði*).

This appears to be the meaning in a well-known tenth-century verse by Thorvald Kodransson, quoted in *Þorvalds þáttr víðförla* and in *Kristni saga* (ch.2). In an eleventh-century verse by Skuli Thorsteinsson, recorded in *Skaldskaparmál* (st.135), the sun is envisaged as a priestess entering the temple (*vé*), and it is probably significant that she is portrayed as the 'wife of Glen'; Glen is otherwise unknown, so it is her status as wife that is important here rather than her relationship to another divinity.

It would be a mistake to imagine that priestesses were a pre-Christian precursor of the vicar's wife, serving mead to the parishioners. Thorvald Kodransson's verse describes how the priestess 'chants from the heathen altar' against him. This description of a priestess is reminiscent of the Irish account of Ota, wife of the Viking leader Turgeis, who 'used to give her answers on the altar in the big church' in Clonmacnois (*Cogadh Gaedhel re Gallaibh*).

These priestesses are clearly engaged in a magico-religious ritual of some kind. In *Ynglinga saga*, we read of a kind of magic called *seiðr*, associated with the goddess Freyja, which was taught specifically to priestesses (ch.7).

Descriptions of *seiðr* usually focus on wandering witches rather than on wealthy priestesses, but just as the priestesses work their magic seated on the altar, these witches always sit on a platform or special seat to perform their magic. Wands and iron staffs are also associated with *seiðr*, and indeed many iron staffs have been found in the graves of high-status women at Birka and other sites; Neil Price has identified more than 30 such staffs dating from the Vendel and Viking eras.

The descriptions of priestesses performing magic are clearly compatible with descriptions of *seiðr*, and in view of this, there seems no reason to doubt the word of *Ynglinga saga* that priestesses were taught *seiðr*. Prophetesses such as Aurinia, Ganna and Veleda (Dio Cassius, *Historia Romana* Bk 67 ch.5; Tacitus, *Historiae* Bk 4 ch.61, Bk 5 ch.22, 24; *Germania*, ch.8), who wielded such influence in Roman-era Germania were also apparently women of rank. The practice of *seiðr* is discussed further in Chapter 5.

Another kind of priestess is found accompanying the wagon idol in *Gunnars þáttr helmings*. She appears to be regarded as the consort of the god she serves, but is not described by the word *gyðja*.

KINGS

If the *goði* held a priestly role on account of his position at the head of his community, so the king, as head of his people, must have held the same role for the nation. As the nation's *pater familias*, the king might be expected to have led the national sacrifice, and *Ynglinga saga* seems to allude to the importance of the king's sacrificial offerings for the wellbeing of the people. Thus, Kings Granmar and On offer sacrifices at Uppsala, when the crops fail King Domaldi steadily increases the value of the offerings, whilst King Olaf the Tree-feller is thought too sparing in his offerings.

However, Tacitus actually contrasts the roles of the king and priest. Thus, while the legal assembly is run by the priests, the king gets only such a hearing as he can win through his personal charisma (*Germania*, ch.11). Although such legal assemblies relied on priests, they clearly didn't rely on kings, whose personal power might conflict with that of the assembly. Indeed, the two most important assemblies were those of the Icelanders and the continental Saxons, and both nations rejected the authority of kings.

Kings could in fact be subject to the will of the people as expressed at the assembly. Thus, the law of the Norwegian Frostathing stipulates that no one may attack another, 'not the king nor anyone else, and if the king does so … he shall be sought out and killed'. King Hakon must obey the will of the assembly and adopt heathen practice

(*Hákonar saga Aðalsteinsfóstra*, ch18), while in *Vita Anskarii* King Eirik declares that he will speak to the assembly on Ansgar's behalf, but that 'public matters of whatever kind are dependent on the whole of the people and not on the king' (ch.26).

This distinction between the king and his chieftains is probably something of a chimera, since it is likely that, at a more local level, chieftains were similarly subject to the will of their leading followers. Although the king might not have ruled directly at his own assembly, he was the patron of the feast, a feast which was held in honour of the gods who were his known ancestors. The great sacrifices, such as those held at Uppsala and Lejre, were thus celebrations of the ruling dynasty's links with divine power. In this, they were occasions to enhance the power of the king as much as occasions for the landowner priests to govern.

CENTRAL PLACES

The sacred grove at Uppsala, site of the sacrifices so vividly described by Adam of Bremen, was at the very heart of the Swedish realm. Similarly, the sacrifice at Lejre was held at the 'chief place in the kingdom', and the grove of the Semnones was clearly central to their nation, since in his description of the sacrifice, Tacitus comments that 'in this, all their superstition looks back as if to the birth of the nation there' (*Germania*, ch.39). Like the grove of the Semnones, where 'deputations gather from all peoples of the same blood', the grove at Uppsala is said in *Heimskringla*, to attract delegates 'from all the Swedish realms' (*Ólafs saga helga*, ch.77).

These were clearly the primary sacred sites of the respective nations. Around the ancient site at Uppsala are the burial mounds of kings, and it is repeatedly referred to by Saxo and Snorri as the principal seat of the Swedish kings. Lejre is not just attested as a central site by Thietmar in his description of the sacrifice there, but also by Saxo, by the twelfth-century *Lejre Chronicle* and by the poem *Grottasöngr*. All these sources associate it with the earliest of the Skjöldung kings, who claimed descent from Odin. Archaeology suggests that Lejre flourished as a royal centre between the seventh and tenth centuries. Another such central site is mentioned in *Egils saga*, which speaks of 'a much celebrated chief temple' at Gaular in Norway, where leading men, including the king, gather from many districts (ch.49).

The five biggest hoards from the bogs of Northern Europe come from Ejsbøl, Nydam and Thorsbjerg on the Jutland peninsular, Vimose on the island of Fyn, and Skedemose on the island of Öland. Each of these lies at the heart of a distinct settlement area, and must have served as a centre for the entire community (*34*).

Thus, the sacred sites which were most honoured tended to occupy a central position in the life of a tribe or kingdom. There were other local shrines, but

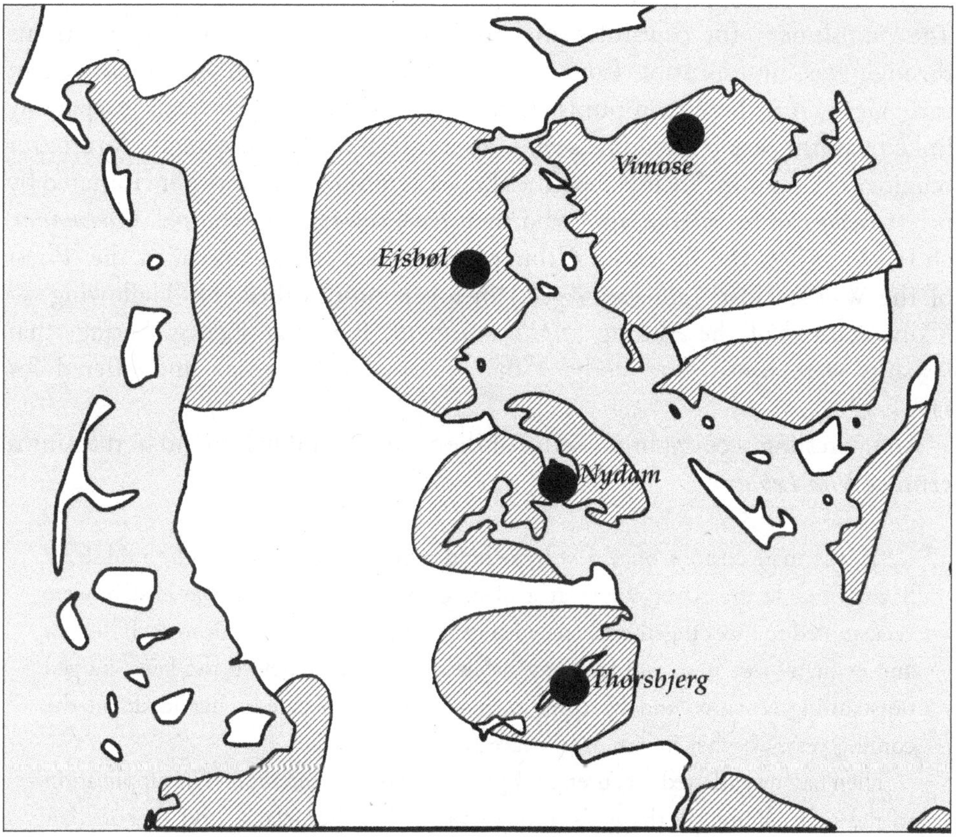

34 Map showing major bog deposits of the Jutland peninsular in relation to the pattern of Iron Age settlement. The bog deposit at Skedemosse seems to have fulfilled a similar central role for the island of Öland. *Based on Todd 1975*

each political unit appears to have focused particular attention upon a single religious centre, which was very often also associated with the seat of power. Place names denoting centres of political power are commonly found in the same areas as names denoting religious centres. Whilst the use of different names shows a distinction between religious and secular functions, their close proximity suggests a close relationship between these two different types of settlement.

SACRIFICE, LAWCOURT, PARLIAMENT, FAIR

> To abandon your shield is a most shameful crime, and the wretch is neither allowed to attend worship nor to enter the assemblies.
>
> *Germania* ch.6

The punishment for cowardice in battle was the loss of a free man's rights through excommunication from both sacrifice and council. In the context of early Germania, these twin punishments would probably have been inseparably linked, as the legal assembly seems also to have been the main forum for religious celebration. Tacitus describes how assemblies (*consilia*) were initiated by priests who call for silence and 'who then have the right to compel' (*Germania*, ch.11). Likewise, the Icelandic Althing was opened by a man called the 'Priest of the Whole Host' (*alls-herjar goði*) in a ceremony called the 'Hallowing' or 'Consecration' of the Althing (*alþingis-helgun*). It was at such gatherings that lawsuits were heard, and perhaps that victims were chosen and offered for sacrifice.

An interesting account of the setup of the Saxon assembly is found in the ninth-century *Vita Lebuini*:

> ... it was their custom once a year to hold a general assembly in the middle of Saxony beside the River Weser at a place called Marklohe. All the leaders were accustomed to meet together there, with twelve picked chieftains from each district and as many free men and as many slaves. There they renewed the laws, judged outstanding lawsuits, and by common consent they decided what to do in the coming year, whether in war or in peace ...
>
> Then having gathered together, they proceeded first to ceremonies in supplication to the gods, suing for the gods' protection of their homeland, and that in that meeting they might make decrees which would be both useful to themselves and pleasing to all gods. Afterwards, arranged in a big circle, they began the meeting.

In Scandinavia, the name for such a meeting is a 'thing' (*þing*). The word seems already to have been known in Roman times, an altar to 'Mars of the Thing' (*Marti Thincso*) having been found at the Roman fort of Housesteads on Hadrian's Wall, dating to the early third century. There were small local things led by one or two local chieftains, as well as large regional or national things, where all the chieftains of the district would be present with their own followers or 'thing-men' from the local assemblies.

There are very clear parallels between the Scandinavian thing and the Saxon assembly. Even the circular formation is confirmed in the law of the Norwegian Gulathing. The procedure is also consistent with what we know of the gathering of the Semnones in their holy grove (*Germania*, ch.39). The account in *Vita Lebuini* goes on to describe the break up of the assembly in terms very similar to those of *Egils saga* (ch.57). The Uppsala Thing (*35*) also formed a circle and its description in *Ólafs saga helga* is comparable to *Vita Lebuini*'s account of the Saxon assembly:

35 Lightning at Uppsala. This nineteenth-century lithograph by Carl Johan Billmark captures the drama of the site, which lay at the heart of pre-Christian Sweden. The current church stands between the burial mounds of kings just as the ancient temple once did. *Uppsala Universitetsbibliotek*

> On the first day that the assembly was seated, King Olaf sat on a throne and his bodyguard (*hirð*) around him. And on the other side of the assembly Earl Rognvald and Thorgny sat on a throne, and before them sat the earl's bodyguard and Thorgny's household (*húskarla-sveit*), and behind the throne stood the peasant delegates all around in a ring.
>
> *Ólafs saga helga*, ch.80

When we think of the Icelandic Althing, of the Norwegian Gulathing and Frostathing, or of the Manx Tynwald, we usually think of something between a parliament and a court of law. This is the overriding impression of the Althing in the Icelandic sagas, where the legal functions of the thing are prominent. Laws are made and lawsuits heard. However the pre-Christian assembly or thing was as much a religious meeting as an administrative or judicial one.

We have seen that chieftains with secular power could also be pre-Christian priests, and that it was these priests who held sway at the legal assemblies. We know that at Norwegian gatherings, the place where the legal committee sat was surrounded by ropes called 'sanctuary bands' (*vé-bönd*). We have seen too that the Forsa Ring lays down that legal fines should be payable to the temple. *Eyrbyggja saga* has told us that people accompanied the temple priest 'just as thing-men do now with their chieftains' (ch.4) and *Hauksbók* explains that everyone 'had to accompany the temple priest to all assemblies …' A meeting conducted by priests within a sanctuary cannot have been a purely secular institution.

Often place names also reveal a connection between thing sites and worship. Thus, there was a legal meeting place at Tislund in Denmark, a name which means 'Tyr's Grove'. In the district of Trögd in Sweden, the thing was held in a grove which stood beside a village called Gåde (from *Gudhø*, 'God Isle') on the island of Enhälga (from *Øin helgha*, 'Isle Holy'). Often place names such as Torsaker ('Thor's Field' or 'Thor's Acre') denote not just an individual field, but an entire hundred (*häräd*) or parish, indicating that the site has had not only religious but also administrative significance.

In *Guta saga* the legal assembly is explicitly connected with sacrifice, in such a way that it appears to have been the main communal sacrificial event. According to the saga, the main sacrifice on the island of Gotland was held for the whole island, with more minor religious celebrations for individual districts:

> The whole country had its highest sacrifice as a nation, but each Third had its own, and the smaller assemblies (*þing*) had lesser sacrifices with animals, food and ale …
>
> *Guta saga*, ch.1

It is implicit in this passage that the most important sacrifice of the Gotlanders was held at their national assembly (*þing*), while district assemblies also held sacrifices. These cannot have been the only times when sacrifice was celebrated and there were probably also smaller community sacrifices at individual temples; certainly, the mid-winter sacrifice must have been a smaller affair, so that everyone could sit in the warmth of one hall together. We have also seen that individuals might offer sacrifice on their own behalf. However, it seems very likely that the assembly had always been a forum for both religious and the secular matters. When the Semnones gathered in their sacred grove, although their proceedings began with a sacrifice, they might have proceeded to affairs which we would count as secular in nature (*Germania*, ch.39); in his *Historiae*, Tacitus describes another meeting in a holy grove, this time between the rebel Civilis and other leaders, but this political meeting was also probably a religious affair (Bk 4 ch.14).

From one perspective, the initial religious sacrifice simply ensures the gods' blessing on the nation's secular transactions which follow. From another perspective, the assembly was the primary religious festival of the nation, which happened to be a convenient occasion to deal with any matters of law or state which had arisen. Neither view really seems to get at the nub of the pre-Christian assembly, in which religion and state are inseparably bound together, just as they are in the priests or chieftains who control it.

Something of the wide-ranging nature of a pre-Christian religious festival is captured in another description of the Uppsala Thing also from *Ólafs saga helga*:

> In Sweden, it was the old custom in heathen times that the principal sacrifice would be at Uppsala in mid-February. Then they would sacrifice for peace and their king's victory; and people would come there from all Swedish realms. And then there would be the 'Thing of all Swedes', and there were markets and fairs, and it lasted a week.
>
> *Ólafs saga helga* ch.77

It is hard to believe that this is the same meeting which was described in tones of horror by Adam of Bremen. In Snorri's account it sounds quite attractive, and events like this were clearly enjoyed by the people who flocked to them. A characteristically earthy attitude to the Gulathing was expressed by Shuttle Halli:

> King Harald went to the Gulathing in the spring, and one day the king asked Halli how he was doing for women at the assembly. Halli answered:
>
> This Gulathing is great;
> We seduce whoever we want to.
>
> *Flateyjarbók, Sneglu-Halla þáttr*, ch.10

SOCIAL SIGNIFICANCE

Festivals were a public celebration of the divine, where the local community or the nation renewed its bonds through shared worship. Religious sacrifice was just one element of such festivals and holidays, which as well as being law courts, parliaments and marketplaces, were also occasions for old friends to drink together, for young couples to meet and for great families to display their power and extend their influence. They were grand parties at which the gods were honoured guests, but where fun could be had by all and bonds of friendship were renewed.

Religious gatherings were not expressions of personal faith, so much as of communal identity. In renewing the people's pact with the divine, they also renewed their sense of community. This sense of the communal is underlined by the role of the local leader, whether king, chieftain or householder, in leading the rite. The celebrations also served to reinforce the social bonds between the chieftain, as host or patron, and his guests or followers. In this way, the gods and the people are joined in a single community. Thus it was the householder's role to feast his family and slaves, and it was the chieftain's role to feast his followers and to provide for the local assembly and its public offerings. Likewise, it was the king's role to provide for the national festivals.

It is in this context that we have to understand a striking story from the Icelandic *Landnámabók*. Two brothers, Ingolf and Hjörleif have made their way to Iceland, where they settle on separate farms. The current text downplays the religious subtext of the tale, but it is clear that while Ingolf sacrifices regularly according to custom, Hjörleif has no interest in sacrifice and lets the custom go unheeded. When Hjörleif's slaves rebel and kill their master, his brother comments that this is what people must expect who do not honour the gods with sacrifice.

Perhaps Ingolf did see Hjörleif's death as a divine punishment for his impiety, but more importantly, he is speaking from a cultural perspective which sees the practice of religion as an inherent part of the functioning of society. Religion was deeply embedded in all aspects of community life. Sacrifice, parliament and lawcourt were all intimately linked, and disregard for one suggested disregard for the whole fabric of society. In neglecting the sacrifices, Hjorleif has neglected the relationship between his household and the gods. As such, not only do his slaves have a real grievance, but the workings of the household have become separated from the divine order, and this estrangement brings about a second breach with divine order in the slaves' revolt.

In this context, Ingolf's comment does not seem so strange or so callous. Hjörleif showed disrespect or disregard for the very foundation of society, and in killing him his slaves follow through a sacrilege which he has begun. Hjörleif has failed to play his part as master, and he reaps the harvest he has sown.

PART 2
ANOTHER SOCIETY

CHAPTER 5
SEERESSES AND SEERS

Religion formed a common bond in Viking and Germanic society. Slaves, farmers, chieftains and kings were all united through their common participation in a shared sacrifice. Yet scattered throughout Norse literature, and from time to time in Anglo-Saxon laws and penitentials, we find traces of people who lived outside the bonds of mainstream society. Thus, in the context of society as described in the previous chapters, these people would seem to have no place in the religious order. Yet although sometimes they seem to be nothing other than beggars and tramps, more often these wayfarers are also magicians and seers or seeresses, and I will argue that they would in fact have played a crucial part in religious ceremony.

In the modern world soothsayers and magicians are perhaps not normally associated with religion, but they deal with objectively similar issues, sometimes in similar ways, and in pre-Christian Europe there appears to have been no absolute distinction between different approaches to the same spiritual world. Indeed, without an understanding of the world of the magician, our picture of pre-Christian religion is only half finished.

These outsider seers visited the houses of ordinary people, who heeded their prophecies and offered payment and hospitality. Thus in seventh-century England, Theodore's *Penitential* rules against 'Those that consult divinations and use them in the pagan manner, or that permit people of that kind into their houses to seek some knowledge ...' (ch.27). In the early eighth-century penitential known as *Discipulus Umbrensium*, we read of those 'who observe auguries, omens or dreams or any other prophecies after the manner of the pagans, or else who bring men of this sort into their houses'. The laws of King Alfred likewise speak of 'the women who are wont to receive spell-workers and illusionists and witches'. The Norse poem *Völuspá* reflects a similar situation, where the legendary seeress Heid goes from house to house and, as in Alfred's laws, it is women who ask her in:

Heid she was called where she came to houses,
a well-foreseeing witch, she knew the spells;
she worked her magic where she could, magic over the mind,
she was always the joy of wicked women.

Völuspá, st.22

WISE WOMEN

In saga accounts, the seeress or witch is represented as a traveller, visiting houses to make prophecies. The classic example is the description of Thorbjörg in *Eiríks saga rauða*, which includes details of the seeress' clothing and equipment:

> She had a blue cloak over her which fastened with toggles and had stones all down to the hem. She had glass beads round her neck. She had a black lambskin hood on her head, with white catskin inside. In her hand she had a staff with a knob on it; it was bound in brass and set with stones below the knob. She had a tinder-belt and on it there was a big pouch made from an animal scrotum; in this she preserved the charms which she needed to have for her magic. She had hairy calfskin shoes on her feet with thongs that were long and tough with big brass knobs on the end. She had catskin gloves on her hands which were white inside and hairy.
>
> *Eiríks saga rauða*, ch.4

Thorbjörg is treated by the household with reverential awe. A high seat is prepared for her with a cushion stuffed with hen feathers and a ritual meal of goat's milk porridge and the hearts of every kind of animal kept on the farm.

Other wandering witches appear in several sagas, such as *Víga Glúms saga* chapter 12, *Örvar Odds saga* chapter 2 and *Hrólfs saga kraka* chapter 3. Going from house to house would appear to have been a feature of their vocation; soon after she has made her prophecies, the seeress Thorbjörg is called to another house (*Eiríks saga rauða*, ch.4). *Sturlu saga* perhaps shows the last pitiful dregs of the tradition when in chapter 7, a farmer fathers a child with a travelling woman called Thordis 'the Liar'. Does her harsh nickname reflect a moralising Christian perspective on the pagan prophecies of the seeress?

The study of pre-Christian magic has attracted a great deal of interest. Particular interest has focused on the kind of magic called *seiðr* (sometimes anglicised as 'seid' or 'seithr'), which is said to have originated with the tribe of gods known as the Vanir. These gods seem to have been fertility deities, and the practice of *seiðr* had sexual overtones. It was taught to the Æsir, the main tribe of gods, by the goddess Freyja (*Ynglinga saga*, ch.4). Freyja herself is a mythological model for the wandering *seiðr*-woman, in that she is said to wander the earth constantly, in search of 'Mind' or 'Spirit' (*Óðr*), which according to Snorri is the name of her husband.

One Anglo-Saxon word for magic was *sīdsa*, which seems to come from the same root as Norse *seiðr*. For the Anglo-Saxons, *sīdsa* was associated with the elves (a variant of the word is found in the compound *ælf-sīden*, meaning 'elf-magic') and recent studies have underlined the identification of elves with the Vanir (see Chapter 7). The Anglo-Saxons had a form of magic which went by the same name and was associated with the same group of mythological beings.

Seiðr is the magic of the travelling seeresses and it seems to have fascinated medieval sagamen almost as much as it fascinates modern commentators. Other magical practices are known from Scandinavian sources, but it is *seiðr* that is especially associated with these door-to-door soothsayers. Whilst the *seiðr* of the Scandinavian sources might broadly be called 'shamanic', it clearly has its own distinctive identity which separates it from better-known shamanic traditions. Indeed, in some respects it is more akin to a spiritualist séance. The seeress seems generally to have sat on a special platform or chair and to have used a staff or wand and a drum. The ritual began with a call to the appropriate spirits, inviting them to participate in the rite. The magic seems to have begun when the seeress yawned, after which questions could be put to her. These questions usually concerned the coming season or the destinies of the young men and women who were there.

Prophecy had to be paid for. As well as food and lodging for herself and her company, the seeress expected a fee, which seems often to have been fairly generous. Notably, the seeress in *Völuspá* stresses who she is making prophecy for and notes that she has received suitable payment from him (st.1, 28-9).

> Host-father chose rings and gems for her:
> he got wise words and the wand of prophecy;
> she saw wide and widely across every world.
>
> *Völuspá*, st.29

In return for payment, there seems to have been an expectation of favourable predictions. In the case of the seeress Oddbjörg in *Víga-Glúms saga*, this seems at first to be an occasion for humour:

> It was generally thought that housewives should give her a good welcome roundabout, since what she said was somewhat influenced by the hospitality she got. She came to Uppsalir and Saldis gave her a good welcome and asked her to foretell something about the boys, and to foretell good.
>
> *Víga-Glúms saga*, ch.12

In this case however, Oddbjörg cannot see as rosy a future as might be hoped for. Saldis gets angry and provokes an outright row, and Oddbjörg predicts utter disaster before she leaves. In the following chapters, the predicted disaster unfolds, but it is hard to escape the suspicion that this might not have happened if the argument with Oddbjörg had not come first.

In *Hrólfs saga* it also seems that a generous gift might have a favourable influence on the prophecy (ch.3). Once she has accepted Signy's gift, the seeress is bound to prophesy in her favour, whereas King Frodi threatens her and is met with ill fortune. Here it seems that the seeress might actually have a role in shaping the future while her prophecy remains genuine; she seems to be striving for a satisfactory answer 'but the *seiðr* was difficult'. It is as if the seeresses have some control over future events, as do the wandering 'norns' in *Nornagests þáttr*, where the 'predictions' are very clearly interpreted as governing future events.

Although I have chosen to use the term 'seeress' to describe these magical women, John McKinnell has shown that there is no absolute distinction in saga literature between the words for women who predict the future and those who shape it (2000). The Norse word *völva* is usually translated as 'seeress', but it can also be used for women who can curse or otherwise shape events. There are also seeresses who are not called *völur*. The terms *spá-kona* ('prophecy woman') and *seið-kona* ('magic woman') appear to be used more-or-less interchangeably with *völva*.

Often, when a seeress' clothing is mentioned, she is wearing either a hooded cloak, or a cloak with a separate hood or head covering. These hooded cloaks worn by seeresses would normally be more appropriate to men, as are the seeress Thorbjörg's hairy calfskin shoes; in only one case (*Laxdæla saga* ch.76) does a seeress wear the sort of hood one would expect for a woman. There might be a purely practical reason for this; these women travelled from house to house about the country and needed clothes to protect them against the weather. Yet the repeated identification of the seeress by her hooded cloak suggests that this garment might also have had ritual significance, a suggestion which seems to be confirmed when Thordis lends her wand and her hooded cowl to Thorkell for him to cast a spell (*Vatnsdæla saga*, ch.44).

Saga descriptions tend to concentrate on a single seeress, but it is possible that larger groups were actually more normal. Thus in *Eiríks saga* the lone seeress Thorbjörg claims to be the last survivor of a group of nine sisters and when she comes to work her magic she relies on the help of others, who form a circle around her chanting spells. *Nornagests þáttr* describes seeresses (here called 'norns', *nornir*) travelling in groups of three, of various ages. In *Örvar Odds saga*, the witch Heid has a retinue of 15 boys and 15 girls who chant for her (ch.2), and in *Orms þáttr Stórolfssonar* a witch goes from farm to farm with her following, giving prophecies (*Flateyjarbók*, *Ólafs saga Tryggvasonar*, ch.414).

The existence of real women fulfilling the role of travelling seeress is widely accepted and relatively uncontroversial. The same cannot be said of the other magical vocations proposed below, but I believe that the travelling seeresses are best understood as one aspect of a larger magical culture which existed in parallel with mainstream Scandinavian and Germanic society.

SEIÐR AND MEN

Ynglinga saga comments on the practice of *seiðr* that 'when this magic is performed, it involves such great *ergi* that it seemed shameful for men to take part in it, and that skill was taught to priestesses' (ch.7). The concept of *ergi* is a tricky one to pin down precisely, but it can imply sexual submission, and as applied to a man, it is associated with passive homosexuality. Thus, to suggest that a man practised *seiðr* would be a slander on a par with portraying him as a female animal such as a bitch or sow. Such insults were not taken light-heartedly and incurred heavy penalties. Other forms of magic, such as blunting weapons, laying curses and reading omens might have been permissible for men, but not *seiðr*. In view of this, *seiðr* has been seen as an almost exclusively female form of magic.

Anglo-Saxon sources, such as Theodore's *Penitential*, King Alfred's laws, or the *Discipulus Umbrensium* (cited above, p.83), do not seem to suggest a particular bias towards female practitioners, even though the provisions of these codes specifically target magicians who go from house to house. However, while Scandinavian literature provides full descriptions of seeresses at work, references to male *seiðr*-workers are relatively few and brief.

The most celebrated example is King Harald Hair-fair's son Rognvald Straight-leg, who was burned and 80 *seiðr*-men with him, by his brother Eirik Blood-axe (*Haralds saga ins hárfagra*, ch.35). Rognvald's grandson Eyvind Well-spring also gathered a retinue of warlocks and *seiðr*-men, and he too fell foul of his king; both he and his followers were drowned by the Christian king Olaf Tryggvason (*Ólafs saga Tryggvasonar*, ch.62). In *Gísla saga*, the magician Thorgrim Nef is said to be 'full of witchcraft and magic, and was as great a *seiðr*-worker as could be' (ch.11). He is employed to curse the saga's central character, and he 'hastens about the *seiðr*, and sets up his equipment after his custom, and makes himself a stage and he works this magic in all its *ergi* and devilry' (ch.18).

These men are all unlike the female *seiðr*-workers in that none of them seems to be a wayfarer. Two of them are closely linked with the Norwegian king, while Thorgrim Nef has his own farm, as do the sons of Kotkel in *Laxdæla saga*; the prevalence of magician farmers seems to be a mainly Icelandic phenomenon, and might reflect the different social conditions of the new land. However when in

Orkneyinga saga, Hakon Paulson travels to Sweden, he meets a male seer (*spámaðr*, ch.36) who seems to be in the same mould as the seeresses. The saga says that he 'would go from feast to feast, telling the farmers how the season would turn out and other matters as well'.

Other male wizards in Norse literature are generally not practising *seiðr*. Many are also foreigners, although this might be no more than a literary device to distance them from mainstream Scandinavian society. The magicians of *Laxdæla saga* come from the Western Isles, and might be of mixed Norse and Scottish ancestry, though their *seiðr* seems similar to that of other sources (ch.35, 37).

The dearth of wandering male *seiðr*-workers in literature contrasts with the emphasis which is placed on the magical nature of the god Odin, who regularly appears as a barefoot walker in a hooded cloak. The unmistakably magical character of this most prominent god is thoroughly infused with *seiðr*, and is a strong hint that, despite taboos against it, male *seiðr* was well known in Viking-age Scandinavia. If the seeresses have a mythological model in Freyja's wanderings, Odin is a perfect model for the sort of roaming magician we are looking for. In the poem *Lokasenna*, he bandies insults with Loki, who also practices *seiðr*, accusing him of bearing children as a woman, 'and I thought that the mark of a pervert (*argr*)'. Loki replies:

> But you worked *seiðr* on the island of Samsø
> and beat on the drum as a witch;
> in the shape of a warlock you went amongst the menfolk
> and I thought that the mark of a pervert!
>
> *Lokasenna*, st.24

HÁVAMÁL

There were clearly mythological models for male magicians in the gods Odin and Loki; there are also convincing references to their existence in saga literature, though fewer than we might expect, especially in the legendary sagas where they ought to be most plentiful. There is however another approach to the subject, which I believe reveals a thriving community of male magicians in the very same texts where we have already looked for them. This depends on a new understanding of the Viking-age poem *Hávamál*.

Hávamál is preserved in a manuscript from thirteenth-century Iceland known as the *Codex Regius*, but like many other poems in this manuscript, it had been passed on by word of mouth for generations before it came to be written down. The poem is a loose collection of verses, most of which fall under the broad heading of 'wisdom poetry'. However, the proverbial statements of *Hávamál* are very diverse. Some ideas recur – don't drink too much; don't talk too much; don't trust too much – but it is impossible to detect any truly consistent theme.

Overall, *Hávamál* is a ragbag of individual verses and longer sequences on diverse subjects in a variety of different metres. Some of the poetic sequences are as brief as two stanzas long, while others would be long enough to stand alone as significant poems in their own right. Many if not all of these sequences and single verses probably date back to pre-Christian times, and most scholars see the poem as largely composed in mainland Scandinavia during the Viking Age. Though there are clearly short verse sequences within it, the first 94 verses are diverse enough to have been largely composed individually according to an established proverbial pattern. Similarities between these verses in both form and content have arisen because they all conform to the same ready-made model, not because they were composed together as a single coherent whole. Verses could be rearranged or omitted, or new verses interpolated without consequence.

All this makes it a wonderful storehouse of quotations, and verses from *Hávamál* are often scattered liberally through works on the Viking Age, as illustrations of characteristically 'Viking' thought. It was just as quotable in medieval times, as a passage in *Fóstbrœðra saga* shows:

> A verse came to his mind then which was said of loose young women:
>
> On a turning wheel their hearts were made;
> fickleness lies in their breast.
>
> *Fóstbrœðra saga*, ch.21

Here it seems that the verse (*Hávamál*, st.84) stands as an independent entity, as something 'which was said of loose women', rather than as a quotation from a complete poem. Snorri also quotes a verse without naming any source and he is usually quite scrupulous in his references (*Gylfaginning*; *Hávamál*, st.1). Each verse of *Hávamál* is a well-crafted epigram, designed to stick in the mind as an independent aphorism, and their collection together into a single long poem is probably a rather later development.

Very many of the verses of *Hávamál* reflect on the world of the traveller. Indeed, the first half has been dubbed 'The Guest's Chapter' (*Gesta þáttr*), though this title gives a false impression of poetic unity. The opening verses of *Hávamál* (st.1-7) show a traveller who has just come to a hall. They raise questions of hospitality and etiquette: Is it safe to go inside? How should a guest behave? How should a host behave? How should one behave among strangers and enemies? These are concerns which the poem will come back to again and again.

Yet despite this interest in the practicalities of the travelling life, it is never great journeys which are undertaken; *Hávamál* is not at all concerned with voyages across the Atlantic, or merchant routes along the Volga, or with any of the other great voyages of trade, exploration and war for which the Vikings are famous. The focus of the poem seems to lie entirely within the Scandinavian world. This unusual interest in the world of the local traveller suggests that many if not all of these verses were composed and preserved by people whose life involved frequent visits to unfamiliar houses within Scandinavia or within a district of Scandinavia.

The title *Hávamál*, is usually translated as 'The Words of the High One', and *Hávi*, meaning 'High' or 'the High One', is one of the many names of Odin. An interest in travel seems apt for a god who frequently appears in sagas and poems in the guise of a barefoot walker, with a staff in his hand and a hooded cloak over his head. No doubt, Odin was dressed in this disguise when he went by the name of Bölverk, a tale alluded to in *Hávamál* (st.104-10) and described more fully in *Skaldskaparmál*, and perhaps when he visited Billing's girl (st.95-101). It is in this guise that he walks through our world, and he not infrequently forms brief associations with mortal men which are recounted in literature.

However, whilst one might expect Odin himself to have been interested in issues pertaining to tramping and travelling, it does not follow that this would have inspired his more settled followers to compose verses full of such incisive comments about life on the road. It is worth quoting a few verses here:

As to his cleverness let no man boast,
But rather be careful in mind,
when wisely and silently he approaches the homestead;
woe will rarely befall the wary.

st.6

Only he who has travelled far and has journeyed much
can know the mind that each man has,
he who is wise in his wits.

st.18

He must go, must not be a guest
always in only one place;
love turns to loathing if you sit too long
upon another man's floor.

st.35

Too early I was in many places,
and much too late in others
the ale was all gone or it wasn't ready;
the time is seldom right for the unwelcome.
st.66

The bulk of the wisdom contained in *Hávamál* is of this down-to-earth and earthly nature, and it only rarely strays into the realms of mystical or arcane knowledge. Many of the verses seem to be sound advice for the traveller, but hardly the sort of wisdom one might expect from a powerful god who has tasted water from the well of wisdom. No other literary references to Odin show the same interest in the specifics of life as a traveller, and it is difficult to imagine their composition and preservation in a society composed of farmers and warriors. It seems most plausible that these verses were the work of real travellers who relied on the hospitality of the settled community, and the wisdom they contain is the fruit of hard-won practical experience.

Very many of the verses of *Hávamál* simply make better sense in the mouth of an earthly wayfarer rather than a heavenly divinity. Could the 'High One' of the title be a man rather than a god? The Norse genitive *háva* could in fact be plural, which would give us 'The Words of the High Ones', or just 'The Words of the High', and perhaps this was a term which was used for an ancient travelling community. As such it might refer to their elevated position on a platform when working *seiðr*.

Another possibility is that it is indeed Odin who is meant in the title, and that the verses of *Hávamál* were associated with real people who lived as the god himself and who walked the earth as his living embodiment. This suggestion challenges our modern distinction between the world of everyday reality and the world of religion. We like our gods to keep to their own world, but in the pre-Christian world, this separation did not exist.

GODS AND MEN

The line between people and gods was certainly blurred in eleventh-century England, where Archbishop Wulfstan legislated specifically against the 'worship of people' (*manweorðunga, Canons of Wulfstan*); the word appears in the middle of a list of magical practices. Wulfstan was Archbishop of York, and his laws and sermons often reflect life in the north of England, where extensive Viking settlement and a century of Viking kingship had all but destroyed the authority of the Church. When Wulfstan speaks of the 'worship of people', he is probably talking about a Scandinavian tradition, which could relate directly to the context of *Hávamál.*

Other Germanic peoples also honoured living people as gods. According to Tacitus, the Germanic prophetess Veleda was 'long honoured as a goddess by many nations' (*Historiae* Bk 4, ch.61). Veleda was a real woman, but due to her power of prophecy she was worshipped as a goddess. We should not be surprised if other magical women and men were similarly regarded.

In an explicitly euhemeristic passage, Saxo describes three races of magicians. The first, who had been of enormous size, are the giants; the second, who practised prophecy through the reading of entrails and what he calls 'the Pythonic art', are the gods. He goes on to describe a third race, arising from the mix of giants and gods, who were less powerful than either giants or gods, but who were still revered as divine by ordinary people (*Gesta Danorum*, Bk 1). This third race of magicians, with no clear mythical precedent, would appear to represent the magicians of the historical past.

What is perhaps most remarkable about Odin's recurrent appearances as a hooded, one-eyed walker, is that he is never recognised by the other characters in the story, until sometimes he reveals his identity through his uncanny knowledge or magical powers. It is often only after he has gone that 'men think it to have been Odin'. Thus in *Reginsmál* and in *Nornagests þáttr*, when Sigurd takes aboard a hooded one-eyed stranger, the storm which threatened to sink his ship abates and he achieves a resounding victory over his enemies; the stranger utters some gnomic verses which would not be out of place in *Hávamál*, but his divine identity is only recognised after he disappears. Less propitiously in *Hrólfs saga kraka*, King Hrolf and his champions fail to recognise their one-eyed host until they have already refused his gifts (ch.46).

These episodes have usually been taken as intrusions of the divine into earthly saga narrative, as an element of 'fictional license'. Every time a one-eyed walker appears with his staff and cloak, we as saga-readers know it to be Odin, and it sometimes seems remarkable that the other saga characters never seem to recognise him. Yet in a world that drew no hard-and-fast distinctions between gods and men, we could in fact be looking at the literary representation of a real phenomenon. Perhaps, these grey beards really did wander the byways of medieval Scandinavia, dispensing their wisdom to heroes and fools alike. If the literary motif of Odin-as-walker reflects genuine pre-Christian tradition, then it would never have been possible to know whether the traveller who called at your door was in reality the god himself.

We have seen above how each godhead could show itself in many different forms, whether sacred trees, idols or sacrificial victims. Thus, when Odin manifests himself on earth it is in no one single guise. There is not one face of Odin, but rather the faces of all his initiates, in whom the god might at any time be present. This is the reason why Odin, of all the gods, has many names. As he says in *Grímnismál* (st.48) 'by one name I have never been known, since I went among the people'. It is surely significant that it is only since he 'went among the people' that he has used many names.

While *Hávamál* might represent the sayings of travelling holy men, in certain passages it clearly also represents the speech of the mythological Odin, and the entire poem would probably have been considered as the creation of Odin, in the shape of his earthly manifestations.

When Odin appears at Geirrod's court in the poem *Grímnismál*, he is 'mistaken' for a magician. Geirrod fails to see the god within the human form. We as readers have made a similar mistake in not seeing the human form that embodies the god.

INITIATION

Medieval art reveals that the hooded cloak and staff adopted by Odin reflect the common dress of wayfarers in the Middle Ages, but if his clothing is unremarkable, his one eye needs rather more explanation.

According to Snorri, Odin gave up his eye in exchange for wisdom. This wisdom was received in the form of a hornful of water from Mimir's Well. The same myth is alluded to in the poem *Völuspá*, where the sacrificial eye is referred to as his 'pledge' (st.28). Such a myth could have reflected, or have been reflected in, a real-world initiation ritual, by which young men were inaugurated into the mysteries of their cult. The sacrifice of the eye and the symbolic drink would have been a precursor to a magical and occult education.

A similar ceremony appears to have been practised on ritual objects too. Thus, on the seventh-century helmet-plaque die from Torslunda, Sweden, the dancer's eye has been deliberately removed (*13*). The object could have been made without an eye, but instead the eye was first made and then removed. Similarly, a pendant head decorated with bird heads from Ribe, Denmark, bears a punch mark on one of its eyes (*36*). An image from mid-eighth-century Staraya Ladoga, Russia, which is also decorated with bird heads, has had its eye removed (*37*), and a similar figure from Uppåkra also has a punch mark on his eye. From Sutton Hoo comes a purse lid, decorated with scenes of a man between two wolf-like beasts; as in the Scandinavian examples, the man has had one eye removed (*38*). The same appears to be true of the little bronze idol from Lindby (*27*). The careful creation of these figures as two-eyed, followed by the ritual removal of a single eye in imitation of the myth is extremely interesting, and it seems highly likely that a similar ritual might have been applied to real people as well as to artistic representations.

Interestingly, the figures from Torslunda, Ribe, Staraya Ladoga and Uppåkra, as well as many other examples, show what is apparently a bird-headed headdress, which Price has convincingly interpreted as a representation of Odin's ravens. However, rather than showing the ravens themselves, these heads are adorned

Above left: 36 Pendant head with bird-headed headdress from Ribe (Jylland, Denmark). It has been deliberately damaged in one eye

Above right: 37 Pendant head with bird-headed headdress from Staraya Ladoga (Volkhovsky, Russia). Like similar images from Torslunda (*13*) and Ribe (*38*), it has been deliberately damaged in one eye

Left: 38 Figure of a man beset by wolves on an purse lid from the rich seventh-century burial at Sutton Hoo (Suffolk, England). Like the figures in bird-headed headdresses (*13*, *37*, *39*) and the bronze image from Lindby (*27*), the man on the purse lid was originally made with two eyes, but one has apparently been removed

with symbolic representations of the ravens in headdress form, as might have been worn by Odin's human representatives . Thus, it is the Odins of this world that are represented in these figures and not the Odin of myth.

Another ritual ordeal seems to be described in *Hávamál*:

I know that I hung on the windy beam
for nights of nine,
gored by the spear and given to Odin,
myself to myself
upon that beam which no one knows
where the roots of it run.

They gave me no bread nor any drink;
I looked below;
I took up the runes, shrieking took them;
I fell back from there.

I took nine power-chants from the famous son
of Bölthorr, Bestla's father,
and a drink I got of the mead so dear,
sprinkled from Soul-stirrer.

Then I took seed and started to grow
and well I was and wise;
word from word led me to word;
deed from deed led me to deed.

Hávamál, st.138-141

The same episode is apparently alluded to in the name of the world tree 'Yggdrasil', which may be translated as 'Ygg's (or Odin's) steed'. Likewise, the Anglo-Saxon *Nine Herbs Charm* refers to Woden as 'hanging in heaven'. In some ways this incident parallels the myth of Odin's eye; it too concerns sacrifice in exchange for wisdom, and once more this wisdom takes liquid form.

SEERS AS PRIESTS

According to Bede, a pre-Christian Anglo-Saxon priest was not allowed to bear arms or to ride a horse (*Historia Ecclesiastica*, Bk 2 ch.13). In his guise as the hooded walker, Odin never rides, and although he does occasionally appear holding a spear

39 Figure of a man in a bird-headed headdress from Ekhammar (Stockholms län, Sweden). He carries a sword by the blade or sheath, as well as a pair of arrows (?), but he is very clearly not wielding these weapons for battle

or a sword, these are never wielded as weapons. Likewise, though the figures in bird-headed headdresses are sometimes shown with weapons in their hands, they are never wielding them; swords, for instance, are always held point down (*39*).

Bede goes on to speak of a priest whom he names as Coifi, a name which Jacob Grimm related to the Gaelic *choibi*, *choibhidh*, meaning 'arch-druid', indicating that Bede's priest was a ritual expert rather than a land-owning patron. The same inference can be taken from Coifi's remark that his services to the gods have done little to increase his worldly riches. After adopting Christianity, Coifi the priest mounts a horse and takes up a spear, deliberately breaking the taboos of priestly behaviour.

According to Tacitus, some Germanic priests dressed as women (*Germania*, ch.43); he associates this with a specific cult, but it is distinctly reminiscent of the practice of *seiðr*. Thus, while the Norse poet Kormak says in a verse that Odin used *seiðr* to woo Rind, the historian Saxo describes how Odin wore women's clothes when he seduced the princess Rinda. Some priests clearly operated according to different rules; Coifi may not bear arms or ride a horse, things which would have been social obligations for men of rank like the chieftain-priests described earlier in the book. The taboos imposed on these pre-Christian priests set them apart from other men. They were not allowed to take part in ordinary manly pursuits, and perhaps for these priests, *ergi* was permitted or even ritually obligatory.

One verse in particular stands out from *Hávamál*, which reads as a catalogue of the skills practised by these ritual specialists. The individual skills cover two general areas of competence: runes and sacrifice.

Do you know how to write; do you know how to read;
do you know how to colour; do you know how to test?
Do you know how to pray; do you know how to sacrifice;
do you know how to dispatch; do you know how to slaughter?

Hávamál, st.144

This verse occurs as part of a description of knowledge gained through the ritual hanging described above (p.95). In this context, the runes are very clearly seen as magical in nature, grasped only through the act of self-sacrifice. There is also perhaps a suggestion that it is only the initiate, who has himself been offered in sacrifice, who is able properly to perform the act of sacrifice. This would appear to confirm that these one-eyed, hooded men had a role as priests. Not as patrons like the *pater familiae*, but as ritual experts who might preside at a sacrifice at the patron's behest.

Bede describes Coifi as a *pontifex* and as *primus pontificum*, comparing him with the guild of Roman priests responsible for conducting sacrifice. As such he is unlikely to have led a wandering life, and although he might have presided at ceremonies in several places, his main temple appears to have been at Goodmanham in East Yorkshire.

Post-Christian law codes contain repeated references to magic and witchcraft, which are denounced as features of paganism. It is easy to dismiss these tracts as simply conflating magic with pre-Christian religion for their own convenience, but perhaps their concentration on magicians genuinely reflects the magician's central role in pre-Christian ceremonies, as the ritual practitioners of the religion. The association of priests with magic occurs in the story of the Anglo-Saxon bishop Wilfrid, when a 'prince of the priests of idolatry' tries to cast a spell against Wilfrid (*Vita Wilfridi*, ch.13).

Scandinavian sources refer occasionally to the role of the 'sacrificial priest' (*blót-goði*), which appears to complement that of the chieftain priest (*goði*). Among the ninth-century Rus, Ibn Rusta perceived sacrifice, if not the whole of religion, to have been under the control of magicians or healers (*atibba*), who clearly wielded considerable power.

They have healers who have authority over their property and are like gods (*arbab*) over them, ordering them to sacrifice … such women, men and livestock as they (the healers) please. When the healers exercise their authority, they have no other option than to comply with the command. The healer takes a man or an animal, throws a rope around his neck and hangs him from a piece of wood until he relinquishes his soul. He then says, 'This is a sacrifice to the God'.

Kitab al-A'laq al-nafisa (adapted from Montgomery's translation)

CHAPTER 6
VALKYRIES AND NORNS

VALKYRIES

Odin's handmaids are the valkyries. Today, they are usually portrayed as beautiful maidens mounted on pure white steeds and clad in shining armour, who sweep up the fallen warriors from the horror of the battlefield. Recent scholarship has challenged this view, and has tended to emphasise the less palatable aspect of the valkyries as wrathful killers. This seems to be how the Anglo-Saxons saw the valkyries, since the word *wælcyrge* is used for the Classical Furies in Anglo-Saxon glossaries. Even so, medieval sources do portray a gentler aspect of the valkyries, and although this gentler image involves some romanticisation, there must have been an original kernel for it to form around.

There is another tradition regarding valkyries, which has also been widely dismissed as romanticisation. This is the idea that the valkyries might be real women. Thus, legendary valkyries such as Hild in the story of the Hjadning Quarrel, Sigrdrifa and Brynhild in the Völsung legends, and Svafa and Sigrun in the Helgi poems, are all indubitably conceived as real women as well as valkyries. Indeed, whenever we meet valkyries outside a purely mythological context, they seem to be real women of flesh and blood.

It must be admitted that all these examples are legendary, but if trustworthy Icelandic references are fewer than we might wish, this might be a function of the peculiar nature of medieval Icelandic society, which was very different to mainland Scandinavian society, or to societies of other overseas settlements. Iceland had no kings and no wars, and without wars, there is no place for valkyries.

In Denmark, Saxo wrote of 'woodland maidens' (*virgines sylvestres*), who seem in every respect to answer to the description of valkyries in other sources. According to his tale, Hotherus is hunting in a wood, when he gets lost in the mist and finds the maidens in their chamber:

> When they greeted him by his right name, he asked who they were. They maintained that it was mainly their guidance and influence that governed the fortunes of war. Often indeed, unseen by all, they shared in battle, and by secret support brought friends the desired victories.
>
> *Gesta Danorum*, Bk 3

Having revealed themselves to him, the maidens vanish. Saxo asserts that the whole scene had been nothing but deception, mockery and illusion, but he leaves Hotherus uncertain as to the reality of the valkyries. Are these real maidens, or are they mere spirits? From one perspective, the question is as phantasmal as its subject. If they are spirits, then they are spirits who can take on human form, and become indistinguishable from real women. If one met a valkyrie, would it be a woman who was claiming to be a spirit, or a spirit who was claiming to be a woman?

Scandinavian sources sometimes seem deliberately enigmatic on this point. Coming from within a society where the existence of real women valkyries might have represented mundane reality, they aim to emphasise the unearthly, quasi-divine nature of these women. The texts we have are complicit in making the myth of the valkyrie, but I believe it is a myth which we were supposed to understand in the context of a world where valkyries really existed.

We are outsiders and to get a clearer picture we must turn to another outsider for help. The eleventh-century jurist Wulfstan, was Archbishop of York from 1003 until his death in 1023. As a representative of the old Christian Anglo-Saxon culture which had been displaced by the Scandinavian invasion, he was very much an outsider living within a pre-Christian world. His is a rare perspective indeed. In his *Sermo Lupi ad Anglos*, he describes a contemporary society of apostates and pagans. In a long list of 'ills', which he believed showed the breakdown of English Christian society, he writes 'here are witches and valkyries'. Wulfstan is unambiguous that valkyries are real and that they have no place in Christian England. Otherworldly beings he might have dismissed either as fictional or as devils, but valkyries are plainly listed among the evils of society. To list a fictional or mythical being would not serve his purpose, which was to reform English society.

Wulfstan was the most trusted counsellor of both King Ethelred and King Cnut. He drafted new laws against paganism, which are quite specific in their provisions. Indeed, he is one of the most reliable witnesses we have, and it is only a shame that he does not tell us more. When Wulfstan lists valkyries as real women and associates them with witches, his testimony should be unimpeachable. Yet all too often his statement is dismissed as casually as if he had written 'Here be dragons'!

However, Wulfstan's evidence is not easily rejected through argument. Indeed, it tallies with evidence from a variety of sources. Writers from Tacitus to Saxo described the presence of women on the Germanic battlefield, urging their menfolk to greater deeds. This female engagement in battle suggests a context in which a more direct magical participation might have developed. If women were already present on the battlefield, then given the Germanic belief that women could be magically gifted, it would perhaps be strange if they did not wield battle magic in some form. *Egils saga* describes how a ritual battlefield was marked out with hazel wands (ch.52), and in such a context, valkyries might easily be imagined to have made their presence known in the battle.

Caesar preserves an account of a kind of battle magic that was practised by Germanic women:

> It was the custom of the Germans that the married women spoke to them from lots and prophecies, whether it were advantageous to join battle or not. They had said this: It is not the will of heaven that the Germans should win, if they went to fight before the new moon.
>
> *De Bello Gallica*, Bk 1 ch.50

Plutarch records the same event, when Ariovistus fails to come to battle, with a somewhat different account of the women's magic noting that the Germanic 'holy women … foretell the future by observing the eddies of rivers, and taking signs from the windings and noise of streams' (*Caesar*, Dryden's translation).

The Anglo-Norman *Gesta Herewardi* also describes women consulting at a well before a battle. This is a twelfth-century tale of the struggle between the Anglo-Saxon Hereward and the Normans around the Isle of Ely. Although the Normans had come to England from France, their Viking ancestors had only settled in Normandy only a hundred and fifty years earlier. Having surrounded the island, the Normans had begun to despair of success, when one Ivo Taillebois declared he knew an old woman who, 'by her art alone could wipe out all their courage and security, and drive them all off the island in dread' (ch.23). Hereward set out to discover what the Normans were up to, and he found lodging at the same house where the witch was staying. The witch spoke in French with the hostess, a widow, about her plans to defeat Hereward's men.

> Then in the middle of the night, Hereward saw them silently go to an east-flowing spring well near the house's garden, so he promptly went after them, where at a distance he heard them talking and questioning, and the replies of some unknown guardian of the spring.
>
> *Gesta Herewardi*, ch.24

Some time later, the Normans are ready to attack:

> … they advanced in full strength to attack the island, setting this aforesaid Pythoness in a high place in their midst, so that, well protected on all sides, she could freely work her art. When she got up, she uttered much scorn and abuse against the island and its people, creating phantasms for their destruction, and afterwards she always ended her speech and spells by showing her nakedness.
>
> *Gesta Herewardi*, ch.25

She performs this ritual three times. The 'high place' is reminiscent of the platform which *seiðr*-workers used and the display of nakedness might echo the description of the witch Ljot in *Vatnsdæla saga*, who 'had pulled her clothes up over her head and was walking backwards with her head stretched down between her legs' (ch.26). Ljot seems surprised that she is spotted by her enemies, and she might have thought herself as invisible as Saxo's woodland maidens; just as the Norman sorceress is supposed to drive off the Saxons 'in dread', Ljot planned that her enemies should have been driven 'mad with fright away out among the wild beasts'.

In *Hrólfs saga kraka*, Queen Skuld works battle magic sitting on a *seiðr*-platform in her black tent at the edge of the battlefield (ch.51); Skuld is a common valkyrie name, which appears in *Völuspá* (st.30) and which can be used as a poetic synonym for valkyrie.

In *Gesta Herewardi*, Ivo claims to have known the old woman for a long time, she speaks in French, and she works her magic in support of the Normans, so it seems likely that she is a Norman herself. Perhaps she maintains a tradition of battle magic handed down from Scandinavian ancestors; if she appeared in a Scandinavian source, this battle sorceress would surely be identified as a valkyrie.

At other times, valkyries appear to have operated from afar. Saxo's woodland maidens are invisibly present on the battlefield. In the narrative poem *Helgakviða Hundingsbana II*, valkyries are seen as earthly women who can ride through air and sea. This should probably be understood to mean that the valkyries are able to send forth their souls, like the magical visitors to Iceland in *Landnámabók* and *Vatnsdæla saga* (ch.12), or in *Óláfs saga Tryggvassonar* (ch.37). *Hávamál* refers to a spell which prevents flying witches from returning to their own bodies (st.155). Likewise, in the Old High German incantation known as the *First Merseburg Charm*, magical women (*idisi*) seem to work their battle magic without the need for a physical presence at the battlefield.

In the Norse vision poem *Darraðarljóð*, valkyries who are seen in Caithness in northern Scotland, seem to influence events at Clontarf in Ireland. These apparitions work as weavers, using a loom on which the weights are human heads and a very similar loom is used by the dream valkyrie in *Jómsvíkinga saga* (ch.7). Likewise, Frankish or German women apparently used weaving in an attempt to assign death through magic; thus in the early eleventh century, Bishop Burchard of Worms asked:

> Have you been present at or consented to the vanities which women practice in their woollen work, in their weaving, who when they begin their weaving hope to be able to bring it about that with incantations and with their actions that the threads of the warp and the weft become so intertwined that unless someone makes use of these other diabolical counter-incantations, he will perish totally? If you have been present or consented, you must do penance for thirty days on bread and water.
>
> *Decretum* (quoted in Meaney, 1981 p.185)

In *Haralds saga Harðráða*, valkyries appear to Harald's men as ghastly troll wives (ch.80, 81). These menacing apparitions show the spirits of the valkyries as they appear to their opponents. The apparent contrast between benign and demonic valkyries is simply a function of which side you happen to be on. If the valkyries are on your side they are lovely maidens, but if they are against you they seem to be foul hags. In *Sörla þáttr*, Freyja takes the valkyrie name Göndull, and appears as a beautiful seductress to the king, until she turns against him when he sees her other face, 'and it seemed to him then to be black and huge'. In an earlier chapter we have considered Freyja as a mythical pattern for the wandering seeress, but sometimes as here, she seems specifically identified with the valkyries. Likewise in *Grímnismál*, she is said to take half the dead from the battlefield for herself (st.14).

It is not a question of whether the valkyries were mythological figures or real women. Not only were they both, they were indivisibly both. Without their ability to straddle both realities, they would have had no special place in either.

NORNS

References to valkyries are scant enough, but they are abundant by comparison with information on the Norns, the Norse Fates. Nonetheless, there is reason and evidence to group these shadowy figures among the supernatural women of this world, rather than relegating them to their grotto beneath the tree Yggdrasil.

Snorri's account of the Norns in his *Edda*, goes beyond our conventional picture of the three mythical Fates beside their well. 'These maidens shape men's lives,' he writes, which is consistent with what we might expect, and is paralleled by the Classical Fates. Yet he adds, 'There are more norns who come to everyone when they are born to shape their lives' (*Gylfaginning*). Thus, Snorri seems to differentiate the norns of myth from other norns who visit newborn children. He continues that good norns shape good lives, 'but as for those men who encounter misfortune, it is because of evil norns'. In a mythical context, this simply doesn't make any sense. Instead, Snorri seems to imply a real-world existence for the Norns.

Clearly, Snorri believed that there were many norns. The writer of the poem *Sigurðarkviða inn skamma* seems to have been of the same opinion, when he makes Brynhild say, 'Ugly norns shaped ills for us' (st.7). Comments like this make little sense unless there are in reality many norns. The same goes for the assertion of *Fafnismál* that the norns come from many different races (st.13, repeated by Snorri), and even perhaps Helgi's implication of the norns in the deaths of Bragi and Högni (*Helgakviða Hundingsbana II*, st.26). Also, in the legendary tale *Hrólfs saga kraka*, where norns are listed among those who are in league with Queen Skuld against her brother Hrolf, these cannot be the three Norns of myth (ch.48).

Perhaps Snorri's most interesting comment is that these other norns visit people when they are born. *Fafnismál* also links norns with childbirth (st.12), and in *Helgakviða Hundingsbana I*, norns visit and shape the fate of newborn Helgi (st.2-4); the same story is also told in *Völsunga saga*, ch.8. Until recent times in Setesdal in Norway, women from neighbouring houses would bring a new mother a bowl of porridge which was called 'the Norns' porridge' (*norna-grautr*). It may be that this continues a tradition which was originally performed by the norns themselves.

The story of Nornagest dates in its current form from the late fourteenth century, and is told in *Nornagests þáttr* in *Flateyjarbók*. Like Helgi, Nornagest is visited at birth by three norns, two of whom grant him gifts of good luck and prosperity, but the third, the youngest, curses him that he will live no longer than the candle that burns by his cradle (ch.11). This is of course, a fictional account and has no pretensions to be otherwise, but the similarities between this account and *Helgakviða* are striking. In *Helgakviða*, the norns bestow only two gifts on the hero, and the same should have been true for Nornagest, except that the youngest norn is angry that she has not been invited to give a gift along with her sisters. According to Snorri, the youngest of the norns was called Skuld, a name which might be translated as 'Debt', and here she seems only to be fulfilling the meaning embodied in her name.

The tale of Nornagest, whose birth is attended by three norns, of whom two bestow blessings and the last a curse, is paralleled by the fairytale story of 'Sleeping Beauty'. Although best known today from Charles Perrault's *Mother Goose Tales*, this story can be traced back to the fourteenth century, when it was the subject of the 'Story of Troïlus and of Zellandine' in the French prose romance *Perceforest*, and it also appears in the slightly later Catalan *Frayre de Joy e Sor de Placer*. The

French romance tale was almost certainly derived from oral tradition, and some time around 1800, the brothers Grimm recorded the tale in German tradition, where it was called 'Briar Rose'. In the earliest version, the 'fairy godmothers' are the goddesses Venus, Lucina and Themis, representing Love, Childbirth and the Law of Nature. Themis doesn't get a gift and so places an unknown curse. Later in the story the girl pricks her finger on a flax spelk, with the inevitable magical consequences. Thus, in this story, Themis is united with her alter ego Nemesis, and Nemesis is equivalent to the Norse Skuld, who plays the same part in *Nornagests þáttr*.

A similar curse occurs in Saxo's *Gesta Danorum*, when King Fridleif takes his son to a temple, where he finds 'three maidens sitting on three seats'; the first two grant charm and generosity, the last grants niggardliness (Bk 6). There is also a Classical analogue for the Nornagest story in the myth of Meleager, who is visited at birth by the Fates who prophecy that he will live no longer than a brand burning in the hearth. The story of Meleager might have influenced the specific curse in *Nornagests þáttr*, but the three Scandinavian examples bear witness to a widespread native tradition, and despite its use of Classical goddesses, the medieval French *Perceforest* has more in common with the Scandinavian tradition than with the Classical.

The motif of the pricked finger which brings down a curse is intriguingly mirrored in the words of Shakespeare's Weird Sisters 'by the pricking of my thumbs, something wicked this way comes'. Whilst a general association with spinning befits otherworldly divinities, the pricked finger might suggest a specific ritual performed by real-world women. The Weird Sisters also have a literary career before the seventeenth century, appearing in Chaucer's *Legend of Good Women* (l.2580), as well as in the earliest version of the Macbeth story, in Andrew Wyntoun's *Orygynale Cronykil of Scotland.*

The Weird Sisters derive their name from Old English *wyrd*, meaning 'fate'. This word is derived from the verb 'to be', and is used to translate Parcae, the word for the Classical Fates. Similarly, *wurt* is used for 'fate' in Old High German, while the Old Norse word *urðr* is the name of the principal Norn. This use of 'weird', which was adopted by Shakespeare, is clearly the origin of our modern adjective, but in this context it apparently functions as a noun. The usage might indeed look back to an archaic grammatical construction whereby 'the three Weird sisters' can mean 'Weird and her two sisters'.

In the early eleventh century, Bishop Burchard of Worms rebuked women for setting three places for the Parcae, who affect a child's future. The bishop seems to be castigating women for a superstitious belief in mythical beings rather than for supporting a continuing cult, but this could reflect an older custom whereby hospitality was extended to real visitors.

40 Dedication to the *Matronae Aufaniae* whose temple was at Nettersheim (Nordrhein-Westfalen, Germany). The figure in the middle is clearly distinguished as a younger unmarried woman

THE MOTHERS

The norns have sometimes been associated with the *Matronae* of earlier Germanic religion; although properly translated as 'Matrons' or 'Married Women', their cult seems to have been the Germanic equivalent of the Romano-Celtic *Matres* or 'Mothers'. The Germanic *Matronae* were honoured in many altars from the Roman era, where they are usually linked with a particular location, probably the site of their temple. Thus, for example, a temple at Nettersheim (near Bonn) contained many dedications to the *Matronae Aufaniae*, while the temple at Pesch (north of Köln) contained dedications to *Matronae Vacallinehae*. The dedications in honour of each group centre on their particular sanctuary.

Worship of the *Matronae* possibly continued in Anglo-Saxon England, where according to Bede, the turn of the year was known as 'Night of the Mothers' (*modraneht*, *De Temporum Ratione* ch.15). This has in turn been linked with the Scandinavian festival of *dísa-blót*, a 'sacrifice for female spirits'.

Whilst it might naturally be supposed that the Mothers were straightforward fertility deities, in fact a more metaphysical concept of motherhood seems to have been equally significant. The Anglo-Saxon 'Night of the Mothers' probably marked the metaphorical 'birth' of the year, while Roman-era altars to the *Matronae* show that their cult included many high-ranking officials and senior army officers, and most of the inscribed dedications were made by men. These well-placed men seem to have been interested in personal achievement and protection. A dedication from

41 Another image of the *Matronae Aufaniae* showing the same distinction between older and younger women. In this image three other figures appear behind the goddesses

Köln shows the Mothers between two Victories standing on globes, while another from Bonn shows a scene of combat between a victorious Roman and an Asiatic barbarian.

A number of images from the Roman Rhineland feature women involved in worship of the *Matronae*. One stone from Bonn shows a procession of ordinary women, while another shows two groups of women who, like the *Matronae* themselves, are bearing baskets of fruit. At Köln, a woman holding a scroll or a baby's napkin (known attributes of the Mothers) seems to be taking part in some ritual. This would seem to be an entirely Germanic iconographical tradition, not to be found on altars of the Celtic *Matres*. Perhaps it emphasises an intimate relationship between the *Matronae* as supernatural powers and their earthly representatives. If so, it suggests Snorri's account of the three supernatural norns and the many others who visit everyone when they are born.

In inscriptions from the second and third centuries, the *Matronae* are ten times called *gabiae* or 'givers', a name which suggests the gifts of talent and luck which are bestowed by the norns in *Helgakviða* and *Nornagests þáttr*. The Norse words *gipta* and *gæfa* both denote luck, but both are derived from the verb *gefa* 'to give', and might represent the belief that luck was the gift of the norns. The Romano-Germanic word *gabiae* comes from the same root, and might reflect the same belief.

The role of the norns, and possibly of the Mothers or *Matronae*, in foretelling or shaping a future for a newborn child or a newborn year is essentially the same role as that of the seeresses who read the futures of the young men and women about the farm, and who foretold the coming season for the farmer. *Nornagests*

42 The *Matronae* represented on a stone from Xanten (Nordrhein-Westfalen, Germany). As with the *Aufaniae*, there is a clear distinction between maiden and mothers

þáttr explicitly describes the travelling norns as seeresses (*völur*) and prophetesses (*spá-konur*). Overall, it seems highly plausible that the norns were also a kind of witch or seeress, and that they also used *seiðr*.

THE MAIDEN NORN

Tellingly, Snorri specifically links the norns directly with the valkyries, saying that Skuld is the youngest norn and that she rides with the valkyries (*Gylfaginning*). This comment can only really be understood if we treat both groups as real women, in which case it might be literally true.

Whereas the norns are associated with motherhood, the valkyries were apparently virginal. Literary valkyries always seem to be unmarried, and sometimes are explicitly identified as such. Thus, Svava, Sigrun and Kara (the valkyries associated with the various heroes called Helgi) are all maidens, as is Sigrdrifa in the story of Sigurd, and Saxo's woodland maidens are also virgins. In the story of Brynhild, the plot turns on the assumption that the life of a valkyrie is incompatible with marriage and the poem *Oddrúnargrátr* draws the contrast (st.15-6). In *Haraldskvæði*, Thorbjörn Hornklofi portrays the valkyrie's virginity as one of her defining characteristics (st.2). This maidenly quality is a sharp contrast with the *ergi* of other groups discussed in this section.

Altars to the *Matronae* from Roman Germania typically depict a young goddess with long uncovered hair, with an older goddess on either side (*40*, *41* & *42*). Her presence is curious because although she is grouped with the *Matronae*, she herself is clearly not a *matrona*, or 'married woman'. This distinction between two older women and one younger is the same as the relationship between the norns in *Nornagests þáttr*. The young virginal 'Mother' presumably fulfils the same role as Snorri's youngest norn. Such an 'apprentice norn' might well have had a distinct role which was less concerned with the rites of childbirth, as Snorri suggests. Interestingly, according to *Nornagests þáttr*, it is the youngest norn who lays a curse on the baby, because she is angry at her exclusion. In purely literary terms, one might expect the oldest woman to have been demonised, since it is usually elderly women who have been portrayed as witches and hags. Yet if the norns had a real role at the birth of a child, perhaps even as midwives, one might reasonably expect that the youngest norn would be excluded from the chamber of the mothers until she had become a real mother herself. It is also appropriate for the valkyrie, the 'chooser of the slain', to utter the curse.

In *Darraðarljóð* and in *Jómsvíkinga saga* (ch.7), valkyries are portrayed as weavers, while in *Helgakviða Hundingsbana I*, the norns spin the thread of Helgi's fate. In a depiction of the *Matronae* from Nettersheim, the central goddess is holding a distaff. These are thin threads to hang an argument on, but it does seem as if the mother norns are spinning the thread which the warlike valkyries weave and cut. Burchard of Worms condemned women for weaving with incantations on the first day of the year, a ritual which might have formed part of the celebration of the Night of the Mothers. Interestingly, the theme of spinning also appears in all the versions of the Sleeping Beauty tale.

Moreover, just as there are obvious links between norns and seeresses, so the role of the norns overlaps with the sphere of the valkyries too. Just as, in *Helgakviða Hundingsbana I*, the fate of the newborn Helgi is shaped by the visiting norns, so in *Helgakviða Hiorvardssonar*, it is only after the valkyries come that his namesake has a name or is able to speak. In *Darraðarljóð*, the magical women seem both to control fate as norns and to intervene in battle as valkyries. Anglo-Saxon sources go so far as to use the word *wælcyrige* to translate Parcae, the name of the Classical Fates.

Ibn Fadlan described the sacrifice of a slave girl as part of the funeral rites of a tenth-century Rus chieftain. He says that the elderly priestess of the Rus was called the 'Angel of Death' (*malak al-mawt*). This phrase derives from the Qur'an, where the angel takes the souls of all humanity to their Creator (*Surah al-Sajdah*, 11), and it also appears in fables where the Angel of Death takes the part played by Death in medieval European stories (as for instance in Al-Ghazali's *Nasihat al-muluk*). Ibn Fadlan might well have chosen the phrase as an approximate equivalent of the Norse word *val-kyrja*, 'valkyrie' or 'chooser of the slain'. However, this old woman accompanied by her two daughters seems more akin to the Norns than to Scandinavian accounts of the young and maidenly valkyries.

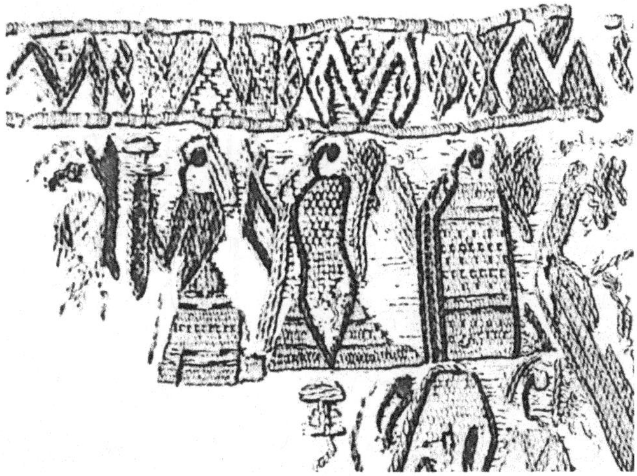

43 Detail of the sacrificial scene from the Oseberg Tapestry (*3*), showing the same distinction between married and unmarried women as on altars to the Romano-German *Matronae*. The leading woman wears her hair loose and carries a sword by the blade. Does this represent three norns, with Skuld the valkyrie in front? *After an illustration by M. Storm*

Ibn Fadlan's is a rare detailed eyewitness account of ritual killing. He observes that it is carried out by a specially appointed individual and that this is a woman. In Roman times, Strabo described the female priestesses of the Cimbri conducting sacrifice by hanging prisoners over huge bowls and slitting their throats. When the blood ran into the bowl, they made a prophecy.

In the top left-hand corner of the sacrificial scene from the Oseberg Tapestry, are three women (*43*). Two are dressed as married women, but the third wears a skirt and short jacket; she has her hair uncovered and is holding a sword by its sheath. Here perhaps, we have a Scandinavian representation of three norns overseeing the sacrifice. The youngest of the three is dressed as a maiden and the sword she carries marks her as a valkyrie. This seems to confirm Snorri's suggestion that the norns began their careers as valkyries.

Like the valkyries and the one-eyed Odinic seers, the norns are neither to be understood simply as ordinary women nor as otherworldly divinities, but as both at the one time. The norns who might come to your door are the earthly embodiment of the Norns who sit at the mythological well *Urðabrunnr*, just as the one-eyed hooded traveller is indeed Odin. In the same way as wandering male seers might have been universally identified with Odin, so in pre-Christian times all wandering seeresses might have been identified with norns or valkyries. In the case of seeresses, however, the waters are murkier, since not only did they apparently continue to operate after the advent of Christianity, but there had always been other women, such as priestesses (*gyðjur*) involved in prophecy.

CHAPTER 7
ANOTHER SOCIETY

All the seeresses stem from Vidolf,
all the warlocks from Vilmeid,
the *seiðr*-workers from Svarthofdi,
all the giants come from Ymir.
Hyndluljóð, st.33

In the foregoing pages, I have argued for the existence of three types of magico-religious practitioner in Viking-age Scandinavia, and suggested that there are hints that similar roles existed in the wider Germanic world. There are obvious similarities and points of contact between these different groups, suggesting that each can be viewed as part of a larger society which operated alongside the mainstream society which has been described in the first part of this book.

In order to accept the existence of this parallel society, it is not necessary to follow all the arguments for the individual magico-religious groups. If, as is widely acknowledged, there were groups of seeresses living outside mainstream society, then there are two basic models possible for their organisation. Either they were virgin orders, and recruited young women who dedicated themselves for life, or they were, to some extent at least, self-perpetuating independent societies.

Seers, seeresses and valkyries are all associated principally with two divinities, Odin and Freyja. Like their followers, both are practitioners of the magical art of *seiðr*, which is thought to have probably entailed a sexual element. *Seiðr* was said to originate among the Vanir gods, who include Freyja as well as her brother Frey and father Njörd; the goddess Nerthus described by Tacitus is related in function and name, and must have been part of the same pantheon. These are the gods of fertility, of wealth and abundance, of growth and fruition and of sex. Freyja herself is the goddess of sexuality. She appears in *Sörla þáttr* as a seductress, and in myth she sleeps with four dwarfs to gain her necklace Brisingamen. The giantess Hyndla taunts her in *Hyndluljóð*, saying: 'You frisk outside at night, Od's lover, like the goat Heidrun would go among the he-goats' (st.46, 47).

Odin is famous for his sexual promiscuity, having countless affairs, apparently with both men and women. In *Harbarðsljóð*, he boasts of sleeping with seven sisters, and later of a 'secret affair' (st.18, 30). Mythical passages in *Hávamál* describe Odin's successes and failures in illicit affairs (st.93-102, 105). In *Lokasenna*, Loki and Odin accuse each other of *ergi* (st.23-4); Loki is said to have borne children, and Odin is said to have 'gone among the menfolk' (*fara yfir ver-þjóð*) just as Heidrun 'goes among the he-goats' (*fara með höfrum*) in *Hyndluljóð*. Although this poem emphasises the *ergi* of these *seiðr*-working gods, they were not solely homosexual; indeed, both Odin and Loki seem to have more sexual relationships with women than with men. However Odin, like Freyja, pursues sex outside the accepted norms of mainstream society.

It is probably this quality of *ergi* that Hjalti Skeggjason criticised in his deliberately blasphemous verse at the Althing:

> I don't want to yap at the gods;
> to me Freyja seems like a bitch.
> It must be one of the two –
> Odin the bitch, or Freyja.

If there were magico-religious cults associated with these divinities, it would be somewhat surprising if they did not also pursue sex outside these accepted norms. Given the strong association between *seiðr* and *ergi*, we can be fairly certain that they did.

The very peripatetic nature of their work has been a cause for speculation over the sexual mores of the Scandinavian seeresses. In 1962 Vilhelm Kiil suggested that the *völur* were in fact ritual prostitutes, but this does not satisfactorily match what we know of their sexual behaviour. Whilst the seeresses were probably promiscuous, they always seem to have remained very much in control of their choice of mate. Such freedom is also explicit in tales of the virginal valkyries, most famously in the story of Brynhild, whose tragedy results from her fury at the deception practised on her to part her from her chosen man. Kiil however, supposed that valkyries slept with young warriors, despite the emphasis which several sources place on their virginity.

A sixteenth-century Norwegian legal case-list translated by Riisøy, notes that 'Men and women who are occupied with soothsaying, runes, heathen chants, white magic who are convicted of infidelity, they are outlawed and the K[ing] and the B[ishop] take their P[ossessions]'. The implication seems to be that such sexual infidelity goes hand-in-hand with their soothsaying.

Price has suggested that one of the powers of *völur* was to make themselves sexually irresistible. In *Völsunga saga*, two women exchange their outward appearance through *seiðr* and each initiates a deceptive sexual encounter, one of which is incestuous (ch.7). In *Hrólfs saga kraka*, King Helgi is unable to resist the allure of an 'elf woman' (ch.15). The *Hávamál* poet boasts that he can use his magic to seduce women.

> This I know sixteenth, if I want a clever mistress
> in all her sense and pleasure,
> I can turn the mind of the white-armed woman
> and utterly alter her heart.
>
> This I know seventeenth, so the young mistress
> will not deny me.
>
> *Hávamál*, st.161, 162

In other passages the poet describes seduction techniques (st.92), and he speaks of the fickleness of women (st.84, 90), before adding that he also has experience of the fickleness of men (st.91). Thus Freyja's reputation for promiscuity, alluded to in Hjalti's mocking verse and in *Hyndluljóð*, might well have been partly based on the behaviour of her initiates. Given the highly sexualised character of their gods, the followers of Odin and Freyja are unlikely to have felt a moral imperative to avoid sexual encounters with willing favourites. This means babies, both boys and girls.

SISTERS AND SONS

I have drawn attention elsewhere (1995) to Welsh and Irish analogues for the myths of Odin and Loki, which place particular emphasis on a man's relationship with his sister's son (and indeed with his maternal uncle), and the same relationship seems to have been significant in the Norse material. Thus, Odin learns spells from his maternal uncle, whom he describes in *Hávamál* as 'the famous son of Bolthör, Bestla's father' (st.140). Tacitus believed that the relationship between a child and its mother's brother was always important for the Germanic people (*Germania*, ch.20), but there seems to have been a particular emphasis on this relationship among magical men.

The importance of this relationship, revealed in Norse and Celtic myths, finds a ready explanation in straightforward practical and social terms, when we stop to consider the consequences of a *seiðr*-based community enjoying illicit sexual relationships across the countryside. Whereas the *seiðr*-man's own children are born and raised (or perhaps, abandoned) in the mainstream community, his sister's children are raised in the *seiðr* community. Thus, the men of the *seiðr* community would have had no children of their own, whilst their sisters' children had no fathers. At a certain age, if we should believe the myths, a boy-child would have been taken under the wing of his mother's brother.

There is another side to the sister's-son relationship which takes on a special importance in relation to the cult of the Vanir. This is the practice of brother-sister marriage. In *Ynglinga saga*, Snorri Sturluson writes that:

> When Njörd was with the Vanir, he was married to his sister because that was their law; their children were Frey and Freyja. But it was forbidden among the Æsir to marry such close relations.
>
> *Ynglinga saga*, ch.4

Snorri's assertion that this was the law of the Vanir suggests he knew of more than this one instance. Freyja's relationship with Frey alluded to in *Lokasenna* (st.32) appears to be extramarital, and both Frey and Freyja are associated with other consorts according to Æsir traditions. It seems plausible that Snorri has in mind the sexual behaviour of a human society, which operated according to the law of the Vanir. In such a case, a maternal uncle might well also be the father.

Illicit and incestuous unions could underlie the unusual wording of two enigmatic verses of *Hávamál*:

> I know the songs that are unknown to the prince's wife
> and to the son of a man.
>
> *Hávamál*, st.146

> This I know, eighteenth, which I never tell
> to maid nor to man's wife …
> but to her alone who is in my arms
> or who is my sister
>
> *Hávamál*, st.163

These verses can be read to mean that the sons of seeresses had no fathers, and that the seer's lover is his sister. In st.163, are the lover in the seer's arms and his sister in fact one and the same person? In st.146, is the song known to a woman who will never marry (a seeress, a valkyrie or a norn) and to a son without a father?

Not all children can have been born of such incestuous unions, and many must have been begotten in the illicit relationships that seem to have been allowed among *seiðr*-workers. Since the male children were adopted by their mother's brother, questions of paternity might not have arisen, and all children born of a Vanir mother would probably have been initiated into the ritual and magical practices of the cult.

ISLAND HOMELANDS

As we have seen, seers and seeresses appear to have lived as wanderers, depending at least in part on the hospitality of their hosts. This cannot hold true for valkyries and sacrificial priests, and these groups must have relied on landed sponsors or patrons. If their services were truly valued then such patronage will not have been hard to come by. Sometimes, in more isolated countries such as Iceland, it might even be that, despite seasonal wanderings, some of the *seiðr*-workers lived relatively settled lives within the larger community.

Nevertheless, if it is to thrive, such a parallel society needs its own homelands outside the realms of mainstream powers and indeed the Vanir and their followers often seem to be associated with islands. The island of Frösö, where Frey's Birch once stood, is one of the two biggest in Lake Storsjön. The other, Norderö is probably named after Njörd or Nerthus. It is to her island sanctuary that the goddess Nerthus returns at the end of her travels, and perhaps such places served as permanent bases for the travelling community. Mainstream society had the mainland, but some of the islands were possibly homes to the *seiðr* folk.

One possible Vanir homeland is the Norwegian island of Tysnes, which was formerly known as *Njarðarlög*, meaning 'the law of Njörd'. It is very likely that this island was once subject to an entirely different legal system to that of the mainland, reflecting the different customs of its inhabitants. Tysnes is littered with many ancient sacred sites; associated local names include Tysnes ('Tyr's Ness'), Vé ('Sanctuary'), Helgasteinn ('Holy Stone'), Goðey ('God Isle') and Vévatn ('Sanctuary Water'). The law of Njörd observed on this island must have endorsed marriages between brothers and sisters, since this was the law of the Vanir by which Njörd had married his own sister. These references to the 'law of the Vanir' and the 'law of Njörd' hint at a completely separate society operating according to its own rules parallel to mainstream society.

Finally, the Andalusian historian Ibn Dihya, writing in the thirteenth century with reference to al-Ghazal's ninth-century journey to a Viking kingdom, associated brother-sister marriage with the continued paganism which survived on offshore islands.

ELVES

The term 'elf' might sometimes have been used to describe all these varieties of wandering magician. For the Anglo-Saxons, the form of magic known as *sīdra* or *sīden* (which was probably similar to the Norse *seiðr*) seems to have been particularly associated with the elves, and indeed the word *sīden* is known only from the compound *ælf-sīden*, 'elf-*sīden*'.

In some Scandinavian sources, the 'elves' seem to be equivalent to the Vanir gods. Thus, in *Lokasenna*, the Æsir and the elves are said to be feasting together (st.2, 13, 30), but the gods named in the poem represent only Æsir and Vanir. In *Grímnismál*, Frey is given Alfheim, or 'Elf-land', as a teething gift (st.5), and he appears to have been seen as the leader of the elves. A religious sacrifice (*álfa-blót*) is held in honour of the elves in Sighvat's *Austrfaravísur*, where Sighvat finds himself barred from a house where the feast is being celebrated.

Elsewhere the word 'elf' seems to represent real people, who might possibly be followers of the Vanir gods. In *Völundarkviða*, the hero Völund appears to be thoroughly human, yet he is referred to as an 'elf prince' (*álfa ljóði*, st.10) and as a 'wise elf' (*vísi álfa*, st.13, 32). Likewise, King Helgi meets a very real elf woman in *Hrólfs saga kraka* (ch.15), and in the same saga Queen Skuld, Helgi's daughter by the elf woman, has the help of elves and norns (ch.48). While the Alfheim of *Grímnismál* looks like a mythological never-never land, in three sagas it appears to be a real kingdom on the modern border between Sweden and Norway (*Ynglinga saga*, *Sögubrot* and *Þorsteins saga Víkingssonar*) and this kingdom is remembered today in the place name Alvheim in Bohuslän, Sweden. *Sögubrot* says that the people of Alfheim were called 'elves' (*álfar*).

This ambiguity as to whether the elves are real people or a category of supernatural being has puzzled many commentators, but it is in fact precisely what we should expect if the human followers of the Vanir are also the living embodiments of the gods. Extraordinary as it seems, it is quite possible that the elves were originally human wayfarers, who only came to be seen as otherworldly spirits after the suppression of their cult by Christianity.

A possible female equivalent to the male *álfr*, or 'elf', is found in the Norse word *dís*. Valkyries are described as battle-*dísir* by the tenth-century Norse poet Thjodolf of Hvin in his shield poem *Haustlöng* (st.17), and as Odin's *dísir* in the anonymous narrative poems *Hamðismál* (st.28) and *Guðrúnarkviða I* (st.19). The German *idisi* of the *First Merseburg Charm* who 'hinder the warriors' also seem to be valkyries. Angry *dísir* cause death in *Hamðismál* and *Grímnismál*, a role which is allotted to the norns elsewhere; in the poem *Sigrdrifumál*, the *dísir* are called on to help with childbirth, and this might also have been a role associated with the norns (st.9). Just as there are many *álfar*, of whom the god Frey seems to be the leader, so there are many *dísir* with the goddess Freyja as 'the great *dís*'; in *Gylfaginning* somewhat confusingly perhaps, she is called the '*dís* of the Vanir' ('Vana-dís', *Gylfaginning* 35). Like the *álfar*, the *dísir* had their own festival, *dísa-blót*.

However, the word *dís* might have had a broader definition, since at times *dísir* appear to be associated with particular families or with the natural environment, and perhaps it is best to understand the word as referring to any female spirit, even perhaps to the inborn feminine spirit of every woman.

GOD-SPRUNG KINGS

Between the two tribes of gods, Odin is the wild card. He is the Æsir god who can behave like the Vanir. He can appear as either the gold-helmed horseman, representing the landed *goði*, or as the barefoot walker, representing the *seiðr*-man. It was from Odin or Woden that the kings of the Danes and English traced their descent. The kings of Norway also looked to Odin as their patron deity, though like the Swedish kings, they also claimed descent from the Vanir in the Yngling line.

John McKinnell highlights a recurrent pattern in the legends of the earliest kings of the Yngling dynasty, whereby kings contract marriages with women from alien magical kindred (2005). Their sons by these women are potentially either like the secular king or like the magical mother and her father. The magical group are seen by McKinnell as 'Winter kings' and the secular group as 'Summer kings', and he links their stories with the mythical marriages of the Vanir gods Njörd and Frey. The same basic legend is told of the kings Fjolnir, Sveigdir, Vanlandi, Visbur, Domaldi, Domar, Dag and Agni in the ninth-century poem *Ynglingatal*, as well as in *Ynglinga saga* and *Historia Norwegiae*.

This general theme of a wedding between a secular king and a magical woman can be found elsewhere too. Thus, King Harald Hair-fair marries the Saami princess Snøfrid, whose father is the magician Svasi (*Haralds saga hins hárfagra*, ch.25), while Harald's son Eirik Blood-axe is said to have found his wife Gunnhild living in a hut with two Saami magicians (ch.34). Likewise, in *Hrólfs saga kraka*, King Hjörvard is married to a magical queen called Skuld, whose mother is an elf (ch.47) and Skuld herself is born through the union of the elf woman with King Helgi (ch.15). King Halfdan the Black married Ragnhild, who was descended from King Alf the Old of Alfheim (*Sögubrot*); Halfdan's father, King Gudrød the Hunter, married Alfhild, who was King Alf's granddaughter, and their son, King Olaf Geirstad-alf was worshipped as an elf after his death. The name of the Danish King Frotho's wife Alvild (Alfhild) suggests a similar elfin origin (*Gesta Danorum*).

In its fullest form, the legend of the marriage between the Summer King and the Winter Princess is mythical rather than historical. Some of the early Yngling kings listed in *Ynglinga saga* might never have actually existed, while other stories might have been reshaped to better fit the myth. However, myths often reflect elements of reality, and the same pattern of marriage between secular and magical dynasties could have been played out in real life. From the evidence of surviving Anglo-Saxon and Scandinavian genealogies, kings were keen to trace their descent from the gods through named male ancestors. Usually, descent was traced back to Woden or Odin. Through a system of intermarriage with a Vanir dynasty, kings would have united two distinct spheres of power, and might have combined patrilineal descent from Odin with matrilineal descent from the Vanir.

Perhaps the woman buried in the great mound at Oseberg in the early ninth century came from such a magical kindred and had married into secular royalty. She was buried with the trappings of secular power, seen in her ship, her sledges and her wagon, as well as her finely made equipment for making tapestries and elaborately woven braids. The textiles buried with her are among the finest known from Viking Scandinavia, including samite and other imported cloths. However, she was also buried with cannabis seeds; her tapestries depicted religious processions, masked performers and hanging victims of sacrifice; the inclusion of her wagon, sledges and ship help associate her with the rites of the Vanir; her apples could be symbolic of the goddess Idun; her wooden trumpet is more likely to have summoned spirits than called warriors. The place name Oseberg might itself reflect her sacred role, since it appears to mean 'Hill of the God'. All these things mean that the lady of Oseberg is now seen as much as a priestess as a queen. A possible analogy to this figure is the Norse queen Ota who fulfilled a religious role and gave prophecies from the altar in Clonmacnois.

Indeed, even the textile-working equipment from Oseberg might have been as much for weaving magic as for weaving cloth. References to woven spells by Burchard of Worms, in *Darraðarljóð* and in *Jómsvíkinga saga* have been cited above. There are also several accounts of magically-woven textiles from Viking Scandinavia. Magical shirts appear in *Orkneyinga saga* (ch.55) and *Örvar-Odds saga* (ch.11-12), while magically-woven banners appear in the Annals of St Neots, *Encomium Emmae* and *Orkneyinga saga* (ch.11). All these magical textiles have been elaborately worked by high-status women, including queens and princesses.

There are occasional hints that there were other sacral aspects to pre-Christian Germanic kingship. In *Haralds saga hins hárfagra*, King Harald is carried about in a wagon (ch.25), and likewise in Einhard's *Vita Karoli*, King Childeric III is drawn in an ox cart; these carriages are reminiscent of the vehicles which carry the images of Nerthus, Frey and Lytir, and which are discussed earlier in this book. In the Norse poem *Rígsþula*, which probably dates from the Viking Age, a knowledge of runic magic seems to be a prerequisite for kingship (st.43-5).

It also seems likely that the early Yngling kings were once routinely sacrificed. *Ynglinga saga* tells how the legendary kings Gudlög and Jorund both die by hanging (ch.26, 28), and King Egil dies with his sacrificial bull (ch.30). King Adils dies at Uppsala during a 'sacrifice to the *dísir*' (*dísablót*) as he rides around the 'hall of the *dísir*' (*dísarsalr*, ch.29). In the case of King Olaf, the saga is more explicit; he is thought too sparing in his offerings, so he is sacrificed himself (ch.47). King Domaldi is sacrificed when the sacrifices he offers are ineffective (ch.15). King On sacrifices his sons for his own continued life (ch.29) and, reading this in the light of all these other apparent royal deaths by sacrifice, it seems that he averts his own sacrifice by offering his sons. The stories of both Domaldi and On are also echoed in *Jómsvíkinga saga* where, after various other offers of sacrifice have been rejected, Earl Hakon sacrifices his young son to maintain his rule over Norway (ch.34).

A FIGHTING CULT

Berserks appear in Old Norse literature as a distinctive warrior type, with their own customs and habits. The earliest reference to them is in Thorbjörn Hornklofi's ninth-century poem *Haraldskvæði*, where the word 'berserk' (*berserkr*) seems to be used interchangeably with another word, meaning 'wolf-coat' (*ulf-héðinn*). Thorbjörn was a poet at the court of King Harald Hair-fair, and in this poem a valkyrie questions a raven about the habits of Harald's court. At first, the raven describes how the berserks took part in the battle of Hafrfjord:

> The berserks howled – battle was on them –
> the wolf-coats yowled and shook their blades.
>
> *Haraldskvæði, st.8*

The valkyrie says:

> I will ask about the berserks' wages, blood-drinking raven:
> What do they win who stride into battle,
> the war-bold warriors?

The raven says:

> They are called 'wolf-coats', who in the fight,
> bear bloody shields, redden spears;
> where they come to battle, they set to together.
> It is daring men, I think, that the sharp-witted king
> keeps with him there, who cut at shields.
>
> *Haraldskvæði*, st.20, 21

Though there might in reality have been a distinction between berserks and wolfcoats, this distinction is not drawn in the poem, which is our only pre-Christian source. Other than the use of the term 'wolfcoats', we learn only that these men scream and howl, shake spears and carry bloody shields. *Ynglinga saga* provides some explanation, identifying berserks as followers of Odin:

> … his men went without armour, and were in a frenzy like dogs or wolves. They bit their shields; they were as strong as bears or bulls. They killed people, but neither fire nor iron worked on them then. That is called 'going berserk'.
>
> *Ynglinga saga*, ch.6

According to *Egils saga*, when men went berserk they became extraordinarily strong, but 'when it was over then they were weaker than usual' (ch.27), and *Hrólfs saga kraka* makes a similar comment. *Egils saga* also suggests that going berserk might involve changing shape, and this idea seems to characterise berserks in many sagas, where they are described as 'shape-changing' (*ham-ramr*). Perhaps, the animal imagery of *Ynglinga saga* alludes to the same quality. Immediately after the description of going berserk, *Ynglinga saga* describes Odin's ability to change his shape:

> Odin changed shape. Then his body lay as if asleep or dead, but he was a bird or an animal, a fish or a snake, and went in an instant to distant lands on his own business or another man's.
>
> *Ynglinga saga*, ch.7

The word *berserkr*, berserk, would appear to mean 'bare-shirt', but it could perhaps be derived from an older root meaning 'bear-shirt'. This second meaning would be parallel to the compound *ulf-héðinn*, meaning 'wolf-coat'. According to *Vatnsdæla saga*, 'those berserks who were called wolf-coats … had wolf jackets for mailshirts' (ch.9). Wolf skins are also worn by Sigmund and his son Sinfjötli in *Völsunga saga*, and they actually become wolves whenever they wear them, even howling instead of speaking (ch.8). There seems to be a real possibility that berserks and wolf-coats were believed in some sense to fight as bears or wolves.

In *Hrólfs saga kraka*, the hero Bödvar Bjarki fights as a bear (ch.33). In the saga, his transformation is achieved in more-or-less the same way that Odin is said to shift shape, and his body stays in a tent while the bear fights in the battle. There are other accounts of human magicians sending forth their spirits in this way. The closest parallel is in *Landnámabók*, where Storolf and Dufthak do battle in animal shape over grazing rights, but here the animals are only visible to a man with second sight, and they fight only against each other. Bödvar's bear is the only instance where a warrior goes to battle in this way, and in fact the saga distinguishes Bödvar from King Hrolf's berserks. It seems unlikely then, that the anomalous details of this story can tell us about how real berserks might have fought.

Part of the tapestry from the Oseberg burial is given over to a battle scene, which includes an animal-headed warrior. This seems to be an artistic representation of the berserk phenomenon, whereby a man takes on the spirit of an animal in battle. On a more literal level, it might simply represent a warrior wearing an animal-skin, like the warriors in Scene 36 of Trajan's Column which have been analysed by Michael Speidel. The Greek historian Leo Diaconus seems actually to have witnessed berserks in action. He writes of a battle against Sviatoslav in 970, where the Rus came on in an extraordinary fury, such as the Greeks had never met with before, fighting without a thought for their own safety and making the cries of wild animals, roaring and howling (*Historia*, Bk 8, 9).

In some sources, shape shifting is achieved through the use of *seiðr*, and it does seem possible that the berserks formed part of the *seiðr*-working community (cf. *Völsunga saga*, ch.7; *Sörla þáttr*). This would help to explain the apparent distaste with which their obvious valour is regarded in the sagas. In later Christian law codes, such as the Icelandic *Grágás*, anyone who went berserk was automatically outlawed, which puts the berserk on a par with the magician or the heathen celebrant.

Berserks were also thought impervious to fire. *Ynglinga saga* says as much (ch.6, see above), and an episode recounted in both *Landnámabók* and *Vatnsdæla saga* tells how two berserks both called Hauk were burnt by fire which had been blessed by Bishop Fridrek. According to *Vatnsdæla saga*, three fires were made inside the hall for them to walk through, and it is possible that this was something of a performance piece, akin to firewalking (ch.46). In *Hrólfs saga kraka*, King Hrolf's men endure an ordeal by fire in the hall of King Adils, after which they throw their shields into the fire, leap through the flames and walk across the coals (ch.41). Odin also endures a fire ordeal in the poem *Grímnismál*, in which he sits between two fires without food or drink.

Like the people of the Vanir tribe, the berserks are depicted as pursuing sex outside the accepted norms, but unlike others they pursue it with force. Thus for instance, in *Grettis saga*, the berserk Snækoll attempts to steal the farmer Einar's wife for his pleasure (ch.40); in *Egils saga*, the berserk Ljot tries to take Fridgeir's sister (ch.65); in *Gísla saga*, the berserk Björn kills Ari to win his wife Ingibjörg (ch.1); in *Vatnsdæla saga*, two berserks are said to be unpopular because they made men give them their wives or money, or fight a duel. There are various other examples in the Icelandic sagas. The legendary Sinfjötli, who like his father takes the shape of a wolf, is Sigmund's son by his own sister.

Interestingly, Sigmund's other son Sigurd appears to inherit the berserks' immunity to fire, since he alone can ride through the flames which surround the valkyrie Brynhild. His story, which might reflect an earlier story about Sigmund and Borghild, centres on his wooing of the valkyrie.

We are unlikely to ever be able to unpick the secrets of the berserks and wolf-coats, but from what little we know, it does seem that we are probably dealing with a warrior cult, which might have been associated with the other cults discussed above. Since the Odinic barefoot seers seem typically to have been older men, it is possible that, just as the norns might have started out as valkyries, some of these grey beards had spent their younger years as berserks.

VANIR AND ÆSIR

> Odin went with an army against the Vanir, but they bore it well and protected their land, and as often as not they won. They harried each other's land and laid it waste. But when they tired of this, they set up a peace meeting between themselves, and made peace and exchanged hostages.
>
> The Vanir sent their most honoured men, Njörd the Rich and his son Frey. And in return the Æsir sent a man called Hœnir and said he was very well suited to be a chieftain; he was a big man and looked very promising; with him the Æsir sent a man called Mimir, the cleverest of men. And the Vanir sent in return the wisest man in their group; he was called Kvasir. And when Hœnir came to the land of the Vanir, he was made a chieftain at once. Mimir gave him all good advice. And when Hœnir was standing at assemblies or meetings, if Mimir was not near and some difficult matter came before him, he always answered the same way: 'Let others decide,' he said.
>
> Then the Vanir suspected that the Æsir had cheated them in the exchange of men. Then they took Mimir and beheaded him and sent the head to the Æsir. Odin took the head and smeared it with herbs so that it would not rot, and said spells over it and gave it the power to speak with him, and it told him many hidden things.
>
> Odin made Njörd and Frey sacrificial priests (*blót-goðar*), and they were *díar* like the Æsir. Njörd's daughter was Freyja. She was a sacrificial priestess (*blót-gyðja*). She first taught *seiðr* to the Æsir, as it was used among the Vanir. When Njörd was with the Vanir, he was married to his sister because that was their law; their children were Frey and Freyja. But it was forbidden among the Æsir to marry such close relations.
>
> *Ynglinga saga*, ch.4

The myth tells us that long ago, the gods of the Æsir went to war with the Vanir, but that the Vanir proved to be a match for them. In the context of these parallel societies, the myth of the war of the gods takes on an extra resonance. The two tribes of gods represent a real division in society, and just as the heavenly war is resolved by a peaceable truce, so too must both the human societies live together.

The minor details have something to tell us too. Hoenir seems to be deliberately contrasted with the 'most honoured men' of the Vanir. As a secular chieftain, he doesn't have to be clever to give judgement as long as he is well counselled. Perhaps there is the implication that, while he might do as a secular chieftain, a *goði*, he would not make a 'sacrificial priest', a *blót-goði*, like Njörd and Frey.

The cleverness of the Æsir is not respected by the Vanir, who try to destroy Mimir. By contrast, the wisdom of the Vanir is employed to benefit the Æsir; the Vanir are given charge of sacrifice and are honoured as *díar*. This unusual term *díar* seems to mean 'priest'. It also occurs a little earlier in the saga:

> In the town was a chieftain who was called Odin. There was a big place of sacrifice. It was the custom there that twelve temple priests (*hof-goðar*) were uppermost. They had to direct sacrifices and to judge men in the assembly. They were called *díar* or *drottnar*. The whole nation had to offer them service and reverence.
>
> *Ynglinga saga*, ch.2

Ynglinga saga is sometimes rather difficult to interpret, because it attempts to treat myths as real history. In this passage, the Æsir are treated as if they are actually priests who offer sacrifice rather than gods who receive it. In this case, the mythological story seems to be an allegory for the real division of priestly roles. The gods of the Æsir represent mainstream society, and the gods of the Vanir represent the *seiðr*-community. According to the saga, before the arrival of the Vanir the responsibility for sacrifice and judgement were united in one man (as described here in ch.2), whereas afterwards the roles were separated so that the Vanir became responsible for sacrifice (ch.4, quoted above). Likewise, as we have seen, the priests of the earthly Vanir community seem to have directed sacrifice on behalf of mainstream society, but legal assemblies were governed by other priests who were also secular lords.

In *Skaldskaparmál*, a slightly different story is told of the peace made between the gods. Here, the Æsir and the Vanir gather round a barrel which they all spit into. From their spittle they make a man called Kvasir, who is 'so clever that no one could ask him anything which he could not answer'. It would seem that, being made from the spittle of all the gods, he has their wisdom too. Kvasir is killed by two dwarfs and his blood is brewed into mead, which Odin goes to some lengths to win from the giant Suttung; in the end he resorts to stealing it. This mead holds the wisdom which had been Kvasir's, and before that had belonged to all the gods, and now this wisdom is distributed by Odin as he chooses among gods and men.

These two myths are both devoted to the same subject, the war between the Æsir and Vanir and the subsequent peace agreement. In both stories, whilst they are equally matched in war, the Æsir win the peace and end up with all the power. In *Ynglinga saga*, they gain the best men of the Vanir, whereas the Vanir send back the only hostage who was worth anything. In *Skaldskaparmál*, the Æsir gain for themselves the wisdom which had come from all the gods, both Æsir and Vanir.

In these myths Odin becomes not just the leader of the Æsir, but of both tribes of gods. He ends up as the sole controller of all the wisdom of the male gods, and he learns female wisdom from Freyja. He rules over 'the most honoured' of the Vanir who must live by Æsir law, and he retains the head of Mimir as his counsellor. He also controls the mead, which contains the wisdom of all the gods, both Æsir and Vanir, and which the poets call 'Odin's gift'. Thus, Odin is no longer simply an Æsir deity but the ruling deity of both tribes and his prominence within the Vanir cult is given a mythological explanation.

In the real world these myths represent a powerful admonition to maintain the status quo. Although the people of the Vanir might sometimes have been viewed with disdain by ordinary people, they had a valuable contribution to make as priests and their powers had been successfully harnessed for the good of the whole community. Toleration and acceptance were profitable, if possibly distasteful. Outright conflict might well turn out badly.

TWIN SOCIETIES

In the second part of this book, we have uncovered evidence for an entirely different society which operated alongside the ordinary society of the pre-Christian Scandinavian world, and probably in other areas of the pre-Christian Germanic world as well. These twin societies were not utterly separate and indeed must have been largely interdependent.

From a modern perspective, the mainstream society looks at first like a fully self-contained secular society. It will perhaps be hard to see how there could have been a role for a second society which seems to have been partially dependent on its more productive secular host. However, in reality secular institutions were identical with their religious institutions to such an extent that the modern distinction between the religious and the secular ceases to be meaningful. Likewise, there is no absolute distinction between objects which exist in this world and the objects of myth. The gods themselves can be embodied in aspects of the landscape, in trees and groves, in wells and fences, in idols and in cairns.

From this perspective, we can see that a parallel society, devoted purely to affairs of magic and religion, might have had a real function, just as medieval Christian society was spiritually dependent on its own religious orders. It is this second society that holds the keys between this world and the world of the gods. Just as the distinction between the secular and the religious breaks down in mainstream society, so in the second Vanir society the distinction between myth and reality also ceases to be meaningful.

Implicit in the Vanir cult (and in its acceptance by mainstream society) is the recognition that it is not the moral laws of society that ultimately keep us alive. Our lives are governed by the indomitable forces of life, death and regeneration, of lust, killing and birth. This is the sphere of the Vanir gods, and the earthly Vanir society operated according to these lawless powers. Perhaps it was the practice of sex outside the taboos of conventional society that allied them with the forces of natural fertility. For its relationship with its gods, for its knowledge of an uncertain future, even perhaps for the continued fruitfulness of the earth, mainstream lawful society was dependent on this parallel society in its midst which operated according to its own very different laws.

However, when Vanir practices were performed outside the province of Vanir society, they represented a threat to social order and were punished accordingly. Thus in *Haralds saga ins hárfagra* ch.35, when King Harald Hair-fair tells him to stop his magic, the peasant Vitgeir replies that farmers' children and farm wives might well practice *seiðr*, since Rognvald Straight-leg, the king's own son does so. Clearly, Vitgeir believes that it is not simply the use of *seiðr* which the king is against, but its use by the wrong people. If mainstream society should adopt the ways of the Vanir, it would quickly fall apart. Vitgeir's remarks provoke King Harald to order his son Rognvald's death.

CONCLUSION

The picture of pre-Christian society drawn here makes quite a different impression from previous assumptions about the function of religion within society. In the first part of this book, I have described a society where religion is so intertwined with the structures of society that it often appears to be impossible to separate the sacred from the secular. This is not to say that secular affairs are dominated by religious considerations or vice versa, but that there is no apparent distinction drawn between spheres which we regard as utterly different.

This first section draws on previous scholarship as well as on a direct reading of primary sources. As such, whilst it certainly includes many new ideas, these tend to be broadly consistent with current thinking about the nature of pre-Christian religion and society. However, the interrelationship between secular and religious worlds has previously been understood in terms of the dominance of one over the other. In particular, it has been argued that laws and legal institutions in pre-Christian society were essentially religious in nature.

In contrast, I have tried to present a coherent picture of a society dominated by powerful landowners, who sponsor religious festivities on their own estates, which double as community festivals, and which consolidate their secular power while gaining them religious prestige. As sponsors and patrons of the sacrificial feast (supplying the animal which is offered to the gods), these men are representatives of the people to the gods, it is they who drink the toasts in honour of the gods, they share their feasting halls with images of the gods, and they are given the title of 'priests'. However, their power is essentially secular, and can be lost and won through conquest or even sold for money. Just as they unite secular and religious roles, the religious gatherings over which these men preside are also secular gatherings where local disputes can be settled.

In the second part of the book, I introduce the notion of another rather different manifestation of priestly power. It is this second part which is likely to be considered the most challenging in relation to contemporary scholarship on the subject. In this section I propose the existence of several distinct but interrelated magico-religious societies, which operated in parallel to mainstream pre-Christian society according to their own laws and customs. The religious authority which these people possess contrasts with their apparent lack of secular authority and prestige, but they occupy the space between the ordinary world and the divine. They represent a very different sort of priesthood to the secular chieftains, one which is based primarily on religious awe and a perception of magical or religious power. In the context of such a parallel society, it is not always possible to distinguish between gods and worshippers.

Some readers might find the idea of magico-religious cults operating within the pre-Christian world rather fanciful. All the more so, since some members of these supposed societies have previously been assumed to have been otherworldly beings. However, I would caution against allowing personal preconceptions based in our modern society from colouring our judgement about what might have been likely in past societies. Similar cultic societies have existed in very many cultures past and present, and there is no inherent reason to assume that pre-Christian Scandinavian and Germanic culture was more like our own than it was like these other more 'exotic' cultures.

Furthermore, if this thesis is to be rejected, it should be in favour of another model which can provide better explanations for the many phenomena which it explains. At present, there is no such alternative explanation even for the social context of the travelling *seiðr*-worker, let alone for the many other loose ends which I have tied off, such as the multitude of norns who visit newborn children, or the proliferation of earthly valkyries, or the many names which Odin has taken since he 'went among the people' (*Grímnismál*, st.48).

If the ideas proposed here are accepted, they have profound implications for our understanding of the pre-Christian religious mentality, and of the nature of pre-Christian society as a whole.

EPILOGUE
RITES OF THE DEAD

Archaeological evidence is at its most tantalising when it comes to graves and funerals. Just as the dead body proclaims the person without disclosing the spirit of life which once gave it meaning and purpose, so the abundant excavated remains of ancient funerals sometimes seem only to reveal the unbridgeable gap which lies between us and the people of the past. We are left with only the physical husk of ceremonies, whose meaning and significance we can only guess at.

On the one hand, funerals allow the living to deal with the physical remains of the dead, and in this context archaeology provides excellent testimony, but funerals also exist on in a variety of non-physical spheres, both social and psychological. Questions of who was present and why, how they were catered for, how they dealt with their loss both emotionally and practically, what they believed of the afterlife and whether they felt able to commune with their gods and their dead, these are not to be answered by analysis of shapes and dimensions of burial mounds.

However, archaeological evidence does allow us to see something of past practices. Sometimes, by reading the physical remains in parallel with written sources, it is possible to deepen our understanding of the pre-Christian experience of death and funeral.

CREMATION AND INHUMATION

Funerals today can be either cremations or burials, and archaeology shows the same division in pre-Christian funerals. After a cremation, the burnt remains seem usually to have been gathered up and buried, so archaeologists distinguish between 'cremation burials' and 'inhumations' (where the body is buried unburnt). According to *Ynglinga saga*, the ashes of the dead could also be scattered on the sea, which would of course leave no trace in the archaeological record (ch.8).

Both cremation and inhumation could be practised side by side within the same community, even within the same cemetery, and this is true of Anglo-Saxon England, Viking Scandinavia and pre-Carolingian Germany. Thus, at the Viking city of Birka in Sweden, where almost half of the estimated 2300 graves have been excavated, they divide roughly equally between inhumations and cremation burials (although the surrounding area leans heavily towards cremation). Yet whilst there are many cemeteries where both cremations and inhumations exist side by side, it is at least as significant that there are others where only one rite was practised. Although the Birka graves were more-or-less equally split between inhumations and cremations, they were often buried in separate cemeteries around the city, or in separate areas of the same cemetery. Similarly, in the Anglo-Saxon cemetery at Spong Hill in Norfolk, the cremations are almost all within the bounds of an ancient enclosure ditch, whilst the 57 inhumations lie outside, a situation which is inverted at Castledyke on Humberside, where the single cremation is relegated to the surrounding ditch.

Cremation is without doubt the older rite among the Germanic peoples. Before the Migration Period, cremation dominated everywhere across the Germanic world, often in vast fields containing sometimes thousands of funerary urns known as 'urn fields' (*44-46*). The earliest inhumation graves appear in the first century BC in Denmark, southern Sweden and the lower Vistula. Yet from the fourth century onwards, Germanic settlers in the empire also adopted inhumation, and in the later Roman Iron Age, the practice of inhumation began to spread through northern and central Europe. By the Migration Period in Germany, inhumation had overtaken cremation as the dominant rite.

LAYING OUT AND BURIAL

After death, the corpse was prepared carefully for burial. *Snorra Edda* tells how their nails were clipped, and *Sigrdrífumál* has more elaborate instructions:

> Bathing makes them ready, those who are corpses;
> Wash them head and hands,
> Comb them and dry them, before they go to the grave,
> And wish them a happy sleep.
>
> *Sigrdrífumál*, st.34

Usually, the dead were laid in their graves on their backs with the arms either laid straight along the sides, or across the body. Other positions are also known, especially curled up on one side in a foetal or half-foetal position. Sometimes it is possible to see that a body has been supported by pillows, or covered by a cloak

44 Anglo-Saxon funerary urn from the grave field at Caistor-by-Norwich (Norfolk, England)

45 Anglo-Saxon funerary urn in the Moyses Hall Museum, Bury St Edmunds (Suffolk, England). Height: 7½in (19cm)

Above: 46 Saxon funerary urn from Wehden (Niedersachsen, Germany). Height: 8½in (21.5cm)

Left: 47 A man sits in a chair on the lid of a funerary urn from Spong Hill (Norfolk, England). Although urns seem often to have been ordinary vessels, perhaps in this unusual example the dead man is represented sitting contemplatively, just as some men were buried sitting in small wooden chambers

or blanket. Perhaps, the different positions of bodies in the grave simply reflect different possible sleeping positions. The graves themselves vary from a mere shallow scoop to a well-dug rectangular pit. At least in England, grave length was not always appropriate for body length, with many graves being either too long or too short for their occupants. Perhaps they had been dug all together at one time, ready for the coming year, or perhaps these discrepancies are simply because the graves were probably dug by family and friends rather than by professional gravediggers.

Many grave pits were lined with wood, and more planks were placed on these over the body before the earth was piled on top. Due to the wooden structure below, the soil would have sat up in a low heap over the grave.

Sometimes larger wooden chambers were built to house the dead. Chamber graves are relatively common at Viking Birka, where they are mainly occupied by wealthy men, accompanied by many possessions, animals and sometimes people. The grave chamber was the size of a small room, between 5ft and 13ft square (1.5-4m), and 3ft to 9ft high (1-3m). Chamber graves are also fairly common in Denmark, but elsewhere they are often associated with royalty, as in the seventh-century Anglo-Saxon example discovered at Prittlewell in 2003, which was 13ft wide and 5ft deep (4m x 1.5m). Inside the chamber, grave goods could be laid out to suggest the sort of living space the person would have known in life. It is probably this kind of grave which is described by Ibn Rusta, who writes:

> When an important one of their number dies, they dig a grave like a wide house for him, in which they place him, putting beside him the clothes of his body, the bracelet of gold which he would wear, much food and jugs of drink, as well as coins.
>
> *Kitab al-A'laq al-nafisa* (Montgomery's translation)

In Scandinavian chamber graves, the body is sometimes seated in a chair, and a seated burial is described in *Njáls saga*, where Gunnar is seen singing happily in his mound (ch.78) (*47*). In a Viking house, chairs were significant pieces of furniture, used only by the householders and their important guests, while other people sat on low benches along the house wall.

In some seventh-century Anglo-Saxon chamber graves, the occupant is resting on a bed, which is often quite elaborately made. So far just 11 'bed burials' are known, mainly from Cambridgeshire and Wiltshire, with another example in Suffolk; the best known is the Wiltshire example from Swallowcliffe Down. Of these 11, seven were certainly female and only one, at Lapwing Hill in Derbyshire, which contained a sword and two spears, appears to have been male. Since the beds in these burials are sometimes recognised from their metal fittings alone, it is possible that bed burials in simple wooden beds have sometimes been overlooked.

As far as we can tell, the dead were similarly laid out whether they were to be burnt or buried. It is of course, much harder to tell from a collection of burnt bone fragments how the dead person had been laid out, but careful analysis suggests that the body was generally arranged on the pyre in much the same way as they would have been laid in their grave for an inhumation. Sometimes, where grave goods have melted in the heat of the pyre and become stuck to an identifiable fragment of bone, it is even possible to see where particular items were placed around the body.

The remains of the pyres themselves are relatively scarce, and it is possible that most cremations were carried out away from the cemetery, perhaps at the home of the dead. However, although the cremated remains were often gathered up to be buried in an urn, sometimes the pyre itself was simply covered over with a low earth mound or even left unburied. At Liebenau in Germany, well-preserved remains from pyres appeared as large round burnt patches, blackened with charcoal and strewn with grave goods. It seems that pots had been ritually broken and thrown onto the pyre either before or during the burning, so that some of the shards were blackened by the flames. After the burning, some of the grave goods, broken pottery and burnt bones had been chosen for burial in a pit, heap or urn, placed either in or near the site of the pyre itself. Similar evidence for pyres has been identified at, among other places, Sancton and Snape in England, and at Birka in Sweden, and similarly burnt pottery has been found in Anglo-Saxon urns at Spong Hill and elsewhere.

BURIAL PLACES

The typical burial site in most areas is a flat cemetery or grave field. At Spong Hill, well over 2000 cremations were buried in a large grave field during the fifth and sixth centuries, along with 57 inhumations. At Sancton, not far from the Northumbrian temple of Goodmanham in Yorkshire, the whole grave field is thought to cover more than 30 acres and to contain thousands of burials, made over a period of 250 years; the earliest excavated burials are all cremations, with inhumations in later graves. In Migration-Period Germany, the commonest form of grave field consists of long clear rows of inhumations known as *Reihengräber*. Some cemeteries seem to have been planned from the outset for the use of generations to come, so the earliest graves are often well distributed, presumably to allow later burials from the same household to be grouped together. Some Scandinavian cemeteries had been in continuous use for as long as 700 years by the end of the Viking Period.

This kind of extensive grave field was known across most of the Germanic territories. However, in the east (especially in Poland) cremated remains might be scattered in a layer on the ground and covered with earth, as at Masłomęcz where the ashes of the dead lay 6in deep (15cm), in a circle 50ft wide (15m); in the middle of this circle wooden posts had marked out a space 6ft x 9ft (2m x 3m), which might have been covered by a canopy.

Scandinavian cemeteries often contain stone 'settings', or alignments of standing stones marking out individual graves. These settings can be circular, rectangular or triangular, and are sometimes filled with stones or earth to give the appearance of a low flat mound or platform; later settings are not filled in and are sometimes made in the outline of a ship. In England, graves were sometimes surrounded by ring-shaped ditches, perhaps with fences, and they might also have little four-cornered houses built over them. Similar 'houses of the dead' are also found in the Netherlands and north-west Germany, where they continue from Roman times up to the Conversion. Good examples come from Apple Down in England, and Oldendorf near Lüneburg in Germany.

From the Migration Period onwards, the flat earthen platforms of earlier Scandinavian cemeteries are replaced by domed burial mounds or barrows. From the Icelandic sagas and from the account of Ibn Fadlan, it seems that these mounds were raised by the mourners themselves. Burial mounds are especially popular in the Mälaren district of central Sweden, and at the Viking town of Birka in Mälaren, they are the commonest type of grave. The mounds are quite low and gently domed, usually less than 3ft high (1m) and 10ft to 20ft wide (3-6m). Over 600 such mounds have been excavated at Birka, of which nearly three-quarters contained cremations; other graves at Birka are more usually inhumations. Usually, the burning appears to have taken place elsewhere, and the cremated remains transferred to the mound, but sometimes, as in Ibn Fadlan's account, the burial mound is apparently built by the mourners directly over the pyre. In Viking mounds at Ingleby, left by the 'Great Army' that raided England in the ninth-century, the lowest layer of earth and stones is blackened with heat, showing that the mound had been built straight on top of the hot embers.

Although most of the Birka mounds contained cremations, mounds with inhumation burials were bigger; the biggest of them were between 15ft and 45ft in diameter (5m to 14m) covering chamber graves. Elsewhere, even larger inhumation mounds have been found. Mounds of more than 65-80ft diameter (20-25m) are classified as 'Great Mounds'. The mounds at Gokstad and Oseberg are 150ft in diameter and 16-20ft high (45 x 5-6m), while the south mound at Jelling is a staggering 230ft wide, with a height of 36ft (70 x 11m). There are about 300 such Great Mounds in western Norway, of which probably three-quarters date from Iron Age to Viking times. These big mounds must have taken a great effort to build. King Herlaug's burial mound in Namdalen, Norway, is said to have taken three years to build (*Egils saga*, ch.3). As well as displaying the power and wealth of the deceased, these large mounds could serve as focal points for later generations, as at Lejre and Uppsala.

The earliest Anglo-Saxon mound burials reused ancient Bronze Age mounds, but from the seventh century onwards, new mounds or barrows were also built. The biggest of these, as at Taplow or Sutton Hoo, are a match for the Scandinavian Great Mounds. However, despite their popularity in Scandinavia and England, in most areas of the Germanic world even simple mounds and barrows are uncommon.

A curious Scandinavian phenomenon is the empty 'burial mound'. Most famously, the mid-sixth-century mound at Raknehaugen in Norway, which at 250ft wide (77m) would qualify as northern Europe's biggest burial mound, apparently contains no burial. Perhaps, such empty mounds were once topped with burials, as was the case at Ulltuna in Sweden, where an eighth-century ship burial was made on top of an empty barrow.

In south-west Norway, such empty mounds are often at the heart of a farmstead, and excavation has revealed plentiful potsherds. Empty mounds in Norrland, Sweden, are often built on top of a contemporary house. Perhaps, these were symbolic hills of the dead; the Icelandic *Landnámabók* records that people believed 'that they would die into the hills'. A particularly striking incident occurs in *Eyrbyggja saga*, when Thorstein Cod-biter dies at sea:

> Thorstein's shepherd went to the sheep north of Helgafell; he saw that the fellside opened up to the north; he saw big fires in the fell and heard great revelling and party hubbub; and as he strained to make out the words, he heard that they were welcoming Thorstein Cod-biter and his crew there, and said that he should sit in the high seat opposite his father.
>
> *Eyrbyggja saga* ch.11

In Ibn Fadlan's account of a Rus funeral, the burial mound is marked with a wooden post, inscribed with the dead man's name. Sometimes such a memorial might have been set in stone, and Danish runestone memorials from Bække and Gunderup, Gørlev and Glavendrup were directly associated with the graves of the dead whom they name. The Gunderup inscription, for example, reads:

> Toki raised these stones to Æbbi his stepfather [?], a good thegn, and to his mother Tofa. They both lie in this mound. Æbbi left Toki his possessions.

The practice of raising a memorial 'staff' as well as stones is specifically mentioned on Swedish runestones from Vreta, Bällsta, Stora Ryttern and Kolsundet. Postholes left by such staffs have sometimes been noted in association with Germanic graves, as in the Viking burial mounds at Balladoole and Ballateare on the Isle of Man, at Anglo-Saxon graves at Portway, Andover, St Peter's Broadstairs and Yeavering, and in or near the remains of continental Saxon pyres at Liebenau. If graves were marked like this in large cemeteries, it would help explain why so few overlap each other.

A stone at Harreby in Denmark bearing the runic inscription *hairulfr* (a man's name) stands just to the west of the prehistoric road *Hærvejen* ('The Army Road'). Similar roadside memorials are referred to in a verse from *Hávamál*, 'Seldom do stones stand by the road, unless raised by kin for kin' (st.72). The Scandinavian standing stones known as *bautasteiner* which carry no inscription, were also probably raised to commemorate the dead, as is suggested in *Ynglinga saga* (ch.7).

BURIALS AT ANCIENT SITES

A quarter of all known Anglo-Saxon burial sites are connected with ancient monuments, usually Bronze-age barrows. Many individual burials were made as secondary deposits in Bronze-age burial mounds, while whole cemeteries sometimes appear to have been sited at or near these earlier burials. The earliest graves are likely to be placed around the barrow, but later burials were made actually in the side of the barrow, while later still, new burial mounds might be built after the prehistoric model. Likewise, among the Alamanni in western Germany, sixth-century grave sites were placed near ancient barrows; in the seventh century, burials were made in the mounds themselves, and in the middle of the century, new burial mounds began to be built. In Denmark, the tenth-century royal monuments at Jelling exploit a pre-existing ancient site, and at Bække a Viking-period ship setting was set up beside two Bronze-age burial mounds, the Klebæk barrows.

In adopting ancient burial grounds and sanctuaries, Germanic peoples seem to have attempted to identify themselves with other more ancient inhabitants. Sometimes, as for instance in early Anglo-Saxon England, Germanic populations were newcomers, who might have been deliberately allying themselves with the local ancestors. Perhaps, as incomers, they felt a particular need to symbolically unite with the indigenous people who had preceded them.

Clearly, there is a possible political dimension here, whereby the invaders impose cultural dominance on places associated with indigenous ancestors. If ancient sites were associated with native ancestor worship or with ancient warrior heroes, pre-Christian settlers might have viewed these sites and their attendant spirits as potential focal points for rebellion. At Balladoole on the Isle of Man, where recent graves appear to have been obliterated by a Viking mound, this sort of interpretation seems very convincing.

However, it would be wrong to read only political messages in the reuse of ancient burial sites. In religious terms, this same act can be seen as forming a sacred bond with the autochthonous ancestors, and this seems a more appropriate reading of sites such as Mill Hill and Buckland in Anglo-Saxon Kent, where Anglo-Saxon graves focus around an ancient Bronze-age burial mound. Set around the ancient barrow, the new burials look almost like retainer burials. Perhaps, the new settlers were offering their own dead as sacrificial retainers for the ancient chieftain, as ambassadors to the indigenous spirits. If the spirits of the ancient dead are friendly towards the spirits of your own dead, they might also look favourably on your community. Otherwise, they might turn against you; the later Anglo-Saxon St Guthlac encountered a hostile host of British-speaking spirits (*Vita Guthlaci*, ch.24).

If such concerns worried the earliest settlers, they seem to have been brushed aside by their descendants. Such links with earlier barrows and other ancient monuments precede the construction of new barrows in the seventh century. At Snape, an early group of Anglo-Saxon cremation burials was set about a Bronze-age mound, but this ancient barrow was later converted to house a larger ship burial, which then formed a focus for a new group of inhumation burials within the old cemetery.

GRAVE GOODS

Perhaps the best known aspect of pre-Christian burial is the custom of leaving objects as 'grave goods' alongside the body. In the late Roman Iron Age and afterwards, rich people were sometimes sent off surrounded by worldly wealth. Archaeologists tend to assume that these 'grave goods' were chosen from among the dead person's possessions, but they might equally have been gifts from family and friends. In Snorri's description of the god Baldr's funeral, Odin places his own ring as a gift beside his son on the pyre (*Gylfaginning*, 49); in Ibn Fadlan's account of a Rus funeral, the dead man's clothes are newly made for the occasion; in the Anglo-Saxon *Beowulf*, Scyld's funeral is supplied with 'gifts' by the mourners (l.43), while Beowulf's pyre is loaded with treasures from the dragon's hoard, which he has not known in life. Clearly, grave goods might also include items which had been personal possessions, but some items at least appear have been utterly new gifts, appropriate to a journey into a new existence.

In truth, such grave goods are very far from being the universal hallmark of a pagan grave that they are popularly imagined to be, though they do represent a

48 This figure on an Anglo-Scandinavian cross shaft from the tenth century shows a man with his weapons laid out around him, just as in pre-Christian burials some men were surrounded by their weapons in the grave. From Middleton (Yorkshire, England)

characteristically pre-Christian aspect of funerary ritual. Many graves held next to nothing in the way of grave goods. These unspectacular graves often go unnoticed, or they are impossible to date, but in Hedeby, a town which existed only during the Viking Age, 95 per cent of the 1500 graves excavated contained no significant grave goods. Flamboyant funerals with abundant grave goods are particularly uncommon in England and Denmark, and in these countries, even where their quality indicates a wealthy individual, grave goods are usually fairly few, often only items of dress and jewellery. If some of the elaborate grave goods found elsewhere were indeed given by the mourners, perhaps this tradition was not so well established in these communities.

Amongst the best known grave goods are the shields and weapons which are sometimes found in men's graves, possibly indicating the burial place of a warrior or war lord; weapons are also occasionally found in women's graves. As well as warrior graves, there are smith graves, containing metalworking tools, usually just a token one or two tools are deposited.

It was very common to bury the dead person with provisions for a meal, and joints of meat together with jars containing food and drink are common grave goods. Bread was found in a clay vessel in an early Vendel grave at Orlunda in Sweden, and bread has been found in Viking-age graves at Ljunga, Västerby i Läby, and in at least 37 graves from Viking Birka. Other foods from Anglo-Saxon and Scandinavian graves include apples, spices, nuts, oysters and eggs; animal bones representing joints of meat are a particularly common find. Scandinavian literary traditions possibly reflect a belief that food and drink in the afterlife can be used again and again, and the provisions contained in the grave might have been thought sufficient for eternity.

Grave goods in cremation burials are slightly different from those in inhumations. Weapons, for instance, are less common. However, small items such as combs and toilet sets, sometimes in miniature form, could be added unburnt to the urn with the cremated remains. As with inhumation burials, the cremated dead might be accompanied on the pyre by animals or by joints of meat. In the urnfields at Spong Hill and Sancton, nearly half the cremation burials featured non-human bone, including goat or sheep, horse, pig, dog, fox, deer, bear, beaver, hare, goose, birds and fish.

RETAINER BURIALS

The most remarkable grave goods are the animals, usually horses and hounds, which were slaughtered to accompany the dead person. Sometimes even people have been slaughtered to augment the burial. Whereas domestic animals (such as goat, sheep, pig or cattle) appear in graves in the form of joints of meat (indicating that these were intended as food), horses, hounds and people are burned or buried whole, and were clearly meant to join their master in the afterlife.

The burial or cremation of animals and people as 'retainer burials' thus seems to reflect a belief that they could be useful or pleasing to the deceased, and the choice of retainer is more likely to have involved sentimental or practical factors than ritual ones. Horses and hounds were especially popular, and some Viking women were apparently buried with their lapdogs. Icelandic graves often included a horse, a hound, or both. The Danish Ladby barrow contained 11 horses and 4 dogs; numerous dogs and horses were also buried at Gokstad and Tune, and in some of the richer graves from Birka. Inhumation burials including dogs and horses are comparatively rare in England. Where horses do occur in Anglo-Saxon graves, they often accompany well-armed men, as in the so-called 'Pioneer' grave at Lakenheath. Sometimes there might be other reasons for co-burial. We can only guess at the story behind a grave at Foulden in England, where an old man was buried with a five-year-old child in his arms and an old lame dog at his feet.

The custom of burning or burial with horses and, in particular, with a wife or slave girl, is referred to repeatedly by Arab writers describing the Rus, including Al Istakhri, Ibn Miskawayh, Al Mas'udi and Ibn Rustah. The most famous account is by Ibn Fadlan, and focuses in detail on the rites surrounding the slave girl's death. After she has resolved to die with her master, she is treated with all the honour due to an important lady until the day of the funeral. Then she goes from tent to tent, having sex with the important guests, who each ask her to tell her master, 'I have done this purely out of love for you'. After this, she is taken onto the dead man's pyre to be killed. Al Mas'udi tells us that if a man died unmarried, he would be 'married after death' so that his new bride could be burned with him, and this scenario seems to explain the elaborate rituals described by Ibn Fadlan.

Al Mas'udi also contrasts the co-burial of women among the Rus with the Indian practice of *suttee*, since Indian women were cremated without their consent whereas the women of the Rus were eager to join their masters in paradise. Both Al Istakhri and Ibn Fadlan confirm that these women went willingly to their deaths. In the most famous example of willing co-burial in literature, the legendary Brynhild achieves in death the wedding she never achieved in life, and gives instructions for a lavish funeral:

> Burn the hero on my left-hand side;
> burn by the hero, on his left-hand side,
> my slave women, bedecked with rings,
> two at his head, and two at his feet,
> two of his hounds, and two of his hawks.
>
> *Sigurðarkviða inn skamma* st.66-7

However, not all such retainer burials were necessarily so willing. *Flateyjarbók* records the story of the Swedish Queen Sigrid who left her husband King Eirik, because she didn't want to die with him (I, 63). At Ballateare on the Isle of Man, a young woman had been felled by a blow to the head from a sharp weapon, before she was laid with her Viking master in an impressive mound; whether she was willing or not we may never know.

Just as men could be accompanied by women in the grave, sometimes a woman's burial seems to have been accompanied by a male retainer. Thus, in a Danish grave at Dråby, a woman's body was accompanied by a beheaded man, and likewise at Gerdrup, a 40-year-old woman was buried in the early Viking Period with a man of similar age whose feet were tied and neck broken. Same-sex retainer burials were also possible, most famously at Oseberg, where a queen or priestess was buried with her maidservant. In a rare Anglo-Saxon double burial at Sewerby, a wealthy young woman was buried in a deep grave, beneath the prone body of an older woman. A grave at Lejre in Denmark held a well-furnished male skeleton accompanied by another which had been beheaded and bound hand and foot. The Icelandic *Landnámabók* tells of the burial of Ásmund Atlason; his slave kills himself and is buried with him, but Ásmund is later heard chanting in his mound that he would be happier on his own; the mound was opened and the slave removed. It could be that this story explains the peculiar dearth of human retainer burials from Iceland.

Sometimes a woman appears to have been buried sitting in the man's lap. This suggests a close physical relationship between the two people, and should perhaps be seen in the context of the Norse euphemism for the sexual act, 'to sit together'. Such an interpretation seems especially likely in view of Ibn Fadlan's tenth-century account of a highly sexualised funeral among the Rus. But whilst in these cases there is clearly a sexual element to the retainer burial, in many other cases there is no reason to assume a sexual component.

Not all double burials suggest a sacrificial 'retainer burial'. A grave at Hestehagen in Norway is thought to have held the remains of a couple who died within a few years of each other, and likewise some of the double graves at Birka seem to have been reopened at a later date to allow the woman's body to be buried with her husband. The same may be true in the case of Æbbi and Tofa's burial mound at Gunderup, mentioned above (p.134).

Sometimes, a single rich burial is surrounded by poorer graves of about the same date, and in these cases it is tempting to assume that the surrounding graves represent the servants and followers of the person buried in the rich central grave. At Köstrup on the Danish island of Fyn, a rich woman had been buried at the heart of a ship-formed setting, with other poorer graves around her. On the same island, another small community of graves framed by a ship-formed setting was found at Glavendrup, which was marked by a memorial to a local chieftain. Perhaps these burials included the remains of some of the people who had laboured to make the monuments.

SHIP BURIALS

The famous Viking practice of ship burning and ship burial has its roots as early as the Roman era (*49*). The grave field at Slusegård on the island of Bornholm, Denmark, was in use throughout the later Roman period and included both cremations and inhumations. Among the 467 inhumations, roughly a tenth had originally contained a complete or partial boat. Since none of these boats used metal, we don't know if some of the cremations had also included boats.

When ship burial appears in Sweden at around the start of the seventh century, it takes on a distinctly aristocratic character. Impressive seventh-century ship burials have been found in Sweden at Vendel, Valsgärde and Tuna, and in England at Sutton Hoo. The earliest Norwegian example, from the eighth century at Avaldsnes, is similarly impressive. These are all extremely well furnished graves, belonging to chieftains or monarchs, and they help to foster the impression that ship burial was the rite of kings. The cemetery at Valsgärde includes a sequence of 25 male chieftains' graves, all inhumations, the earlier ones buried in small chamber graves, the later ones in ship graves; there are also about 50 cremation

49 Ships begin to feature prominently on Gotland stones at more-or-less the time that ship burials become prominent in Scandinavian archaeology. This stone is from Lärbro Tängelgårda

graves, nearly all women. This situation is reversed 40 miles away (70km) at Tuna, where the grave field contains a number of well-furnished female burials, including 8 ship burials, as well as a large number of male cremations.

Elaborate Viking ship burials at Oseberg, Gokstad, Ladby, Hedeby and Île de Groix underline the aristocratic associations of the rite, but not all ship burials are high status, and elsewhere people could be buried in little fishing boats or dugout canoes. In Ibn Fadlan's account of a tenth-century ship burning, he states that 'In the case of a poor man, they build a small boat, place him inside and burn it' (Montgomery's translation). At Birka, 285 cremation burials contained clench nails of a kind normally used in ship-building and in the Viking graves at Ingleby in England, small numbers of clench nails are present in five of the six excavated cremation burials. These might represent a deliberate token use of boat parts in the funeral ritual as a substitute for a complete vessel. Likewise, at Kaupang, in the crowded Bikholberg gravefield, some graves contained only parts of ships while others had complete vessels of various sizes.

Ship burial does seem to be a peculiarly Scandinavian phenomenon. Boat burials outside Scandinavia are unusual, and where they do occur, as at Île de Groix in France, or Sutton Hoo in England, they are generally associated with other distinctively Scandinavian artefacts. The rite also seems to have taken many different forms: ship burials exist both as cremations and as inhumations, in lone burial mounds or in extensive grave fields; they can be upside down or the right way up; sometimes the boat is moored in the burial mound as at Oseberg, sometimes it is ready to sail with its anchor aboard as at Ladby; in *Beowulf*, the body of the Danish king Scyld is set adrift on a ship laden with gifts, while in *Ynglinga saga*, King Haki's ship is set afire on the water (ch.27); some burials include only parts of ships, and some do not include ships at all, but merely the shape of a ship outlined in stones.

It might be significant that Odin sometimes appears as a ferryman in Scandinavian sources. Thus, in the *Codex Regius* prose passage 'On the death of Sinfjötli', the hero Sigmund carries his son's body to the edge of a fjord:

> There was a little boat there and a man in it. He offered to take Sigmund over the fjord. But after Sigmund carried the corpse out onto the ship, the boat was fully laden. The man told Sigmund to walk round the fjord. The man pushed the boat out, and then he vanished.
>
> *Frá dauða Sinfjötla*

WAGON BURIALS

There is also a small but significant group of wagon graves from Viking Scandinavia. These are mainly chamber graves from tenth-century Denmark, although the most famous, the Oseberg burial (which is also a boat grave), is from ninth-century Norway. There is another wagon burial in grave Bj.1131 at Birka in Sweden. However, most of the wagon graves come from Denmark and North Germany. In only three cases is the sex of the occupant unknown; the rest are all women's graves. This is very different from the situation with regard to boat burials, where although there are local variations, there is no clear overall sexual bias.

Another curious feature of the wagon graves is that, whereas many of them can be quite rich in artefacts, none of them has so far been found to contain the twin oval brooches which often form the most distinctive feature of a Viking woman's burial goods. I have argued elsewhere (2006) that the presence of these brooches in an inhumation might indicate the grave of a married wife, and so their absence from the nearly 20 wagon graves is a good indication that we are probably dealing with a specific group of unmarried women. In some cases, notably at Fyrkat and Oseberg, the grave goods include what appear to be ritual and magical apparatus, raising the possibility that these were women who pursued magic rather than marriage. The close association of wagons with religious rituals and in particular with the Vanir, has been noted already. An early Celtic wagon grave at Vix in France has also been interpreted as the grave of a priestess or seeress, buried in her wagon with an enormous vessel for sacrificial blood. However, in Denmark, these graves have more often been seen as proto-Christian burials.

A wagon grave from Hørning might once have been a focus for local veneration, or at least superstitious awe. The mound had been built over a sunken chamber grave containing the body of woman buried with a wagon and many other grave goods, which suggest a date in the late tenth or early eleventh centuries. Shortly after 1060, the mound was demolished and replaced with a Christian church. Although the Hørning woman has usually been interpreted as an early Christian whose memory was honoured by later church-builders, it is perhaps more likely that her barrow had become a focus for rituals in her honour, and the church was built here to supplant a pre-Christian religious site, just as holy trees were replaced by churches at Gaesmere and Frösö (see above, p.46). We have seen that seeresses could be regarded as semi-divine in their own lifetime, so if the woman buried here was a seeress, she might have been especially likely to have attracted a cult after her death. In *Laxdæla saga*, we read of a church built over the grave of a seeress, although here the bones are later dug up and disposed of (ch.76).

There is some evidence to suggest that the wagon grave at Fyrkat (which included narcotics and possible religious paraphernalia) might also have been a focus of unusual attention. In *Baldrs draumar*, Odin raises an unwilling seeress from the grave, and the same scenario seems to underlie *Völuspá*; likewise, in *Grógaldr*, Svipdag raises his mother, the seeress Groa from her grave. Given the attention that seeresses' graves received in literature, it should not be surprising if we find that they attracted ritual activity in historical reality.

A rare literary glimpse of a wagon funeral occurs in the *Codex Regius*, where the prose introduction to *Helreið Brynhildar* describes the double cremation held for Sigurd and Brynhild:

> After the death of Brynhild, two pyres were made; one for Sigurd and that burnt first, but Brynhild was burnt on the other, and she was in a wagon and it was draped with samite. It is said, that Brynhild drove the wagon on the road to Hel …
>
> *Helreið Brynhildar*, prose introduction

Interestingly, Brynhild and her wagon are cremated and so her grave would be unrecognisable as a wagon grave in the archaeological record. There could potentially be countless such wagon cremations, which have not been identified. It might also be significant, in view of the possible association of wagon burials with unmarried magical women, that Brynhild had originally been a valkyrie, a role which is explicitly linked in her story with unmarried status.

INVERTED WEAPONS

In Viking graves, weapons are not always laid out alongside the other grave goods as one might expect, but sometimes appear to have been cast or thrust into the grave over the bodies of the dead. Likewise, in cremation burials, weapons are sometimes thrust vertically downwards, through the cremated remains. Recently, Andreas Nordberg has noted 19 examples of weapons deposited in this way, and Neil Price has drawn attention to four examples from Birka, making a total of 15 swords, 15 spears and 15 axes embedded in Viking graves.

Thus, at Klinta on the Swedish island of Öland, a sword was placed point down into the ashes of a male cremation burial. In a rich double grave at Birka (Bj.834), a spearhead was found embedded in the wooden planking surrounding the main burial. It had apparently been thrown over the dead couple with some force, and had penetrated the wood to a depth of 1ft (30cm), so that only 6in (15cm) of iron protruded. Another example, not noted by Price or Nordberg, comes from Jurby on the Isle of Man, where two spears had been thrown into the backfill of the pit, where they had lodged only 2ft 8in (80cm) below the ground surface. Unless the spear shafts were deliberately broken off, they must have stuck out of the grave for many years after the burial.

Scattered literary references seem to link these embedded weapons with dedication to the god Odin. Odin himself is marked with the spear in *Hávamál* (st.137); likewise, in *Víkarsbálkr*, Starkad offers Vikar to the gods by thrusting a spear into his heart (st.20), and in the acompanying prose of *Gautreks saga* he uses the words, 'Now I give you to Odin' (ch.7). In the medieval Icelandic story *Styrbjarnar þáttr Svíakappa* (*Flateyjarbók* II, 61), King Eiríkr hurls a spear over his enemy with the words 'Odin owns you all'. This same practice of casting a spear over the enemy in dedication to Odin is alluded to in the poems *Völuspá* (st.24) and *Hlöðskviða* (st.28). It would seem that a sacrificial ritual has been extended to the rites of battle and burial (*50*). In *Ynglinga saga*, as in *Hávamál*, Odin is marked with the spear, but in the saga account he is portrayed as a human chieftain, who asks to be marked at the point of death so that he can join the gods when he dies (ch.9).

HONOURING THE DEAD

The funeral itself seems to have included not only the cremation or interment, but also where appropriate the making of the burial mound. *Gísla saga*, which is set in tenth-century Iceland, includes two funerals, both of which are called 'mound-makings'; after the burial, they go back to the house to drink the funeral ale. Presumably, there are far more people present than the relatives and close

50 On the same stone from Lärbro Tängelgårda, Gotland, a procession of men hold their down-pointed swords by the hilt; behind them, an eight-legged horse carries away a prostrate figure. The men are probably taking part in a funeral, while the magical horse carries the dead man away to the otherworld. The symbolism of inverted weapons is also found in Viking graves

friends named in the saga, so that in one case the funeral is jointly organised by two households, each holding a separate funeral ale (ch.14, 17). Gifts were distributed among the guests (ch.18, *Laxdæla saga* ch.27). Obviously, a little time must have been allowed for everyone to gather; in Ibn Fadlan's account of a tenth-century Rus funeral, the body is initially buried, then 10 days later it is exhumed for cremation.

Late Anglo-Saxon documents detail provisions and expenses incurred at funerals, showing that ale remained as an important element of the feast even after the introduction of Christianity. More provisions are laid in for a second memorial feast a month later, and this was clearly a more elaborate affair. Hoskuld's extravagant funeral feast in *Laxdæla saga* (ch.26-7) is held several months after his death, allowing time for the huge number of guests to gather. This feast lasts for two weeks and is clearly as much an occasion for extending the influence of his descendants as for honouring his memory. However, the saga writer suggests that this was something of a novel fashion, and might derive ultimately from Roman custom introduced via Christian England.

The Carolingian *Indiculus Superstitionum et Paganiarum* begins with two provisions against pre-Christian practices in honour of the dead:

1. Of sacrilege at the tombs of the dead
2. Of sacrilege over the deceased, that is '*dadsisas*'

The nature of these *dadsisas* might be revealed by two further provisions, which taken together suggest that sacrifice might be offered to the dead:

9. Of the sacrifice which is offered to any of the saints.

25. Of this, that they feign for themselves that dead persons of whatever sort are saints.

A recent study of later Iron-age burial customs in Halland, Sweden, notes that animal bones and potsherds have often been found close to the surface of graves. At Laverstock in England, pottery seems to have been dropped into a seventh-century barrow after the burial, perhaps suggesting that food or drink might have been left, in much the same way that people lay flowers on graves today.

Anne Sofie Gräslund has drawn attention to external kists or pits, often containing pottery and animal bones, which are associated with Viking-era burials across Sweden. Usually, these kists lie to the south or west of the burial, well over half of them lie due south-west. One might imagine a meal by the setting sun (thus the south-westerly orientation) in which food and drink was shared with the occupants of the mound or grave. Several old Scandinavian lawcodes forbade sacrifice at burial mounds, and as late as 1659, a synod at Visby exhorted the clergy to stop farmers from 'sacrificing at the graves of the departed'. Nineteenth-century Swedish tradition remembered the offering of Yule beer at mounds and cemeteries, and offerings of sandwiches and aquavit have been observed in more recent times.

Sharing a meal with an honoured forebear is a practice akin to sacrifice, and such a relationship with the dead would commonly be termed 'ancestor worship'. In some cases there seems to be evidence that this could extend beyond simply honouring the memory of the dead into something more akin to religious devotion. According to *Óláfs þáttr Geirstaðaálfs* (*Flateyjarbók* II, 3-9) and *Ynglinga saga* (ch.53-4), the Norwegian king Olaf, whose reign had been blessed with good harvests, was buried in a mound at Geirstad where the people made offerings to him, and he was known after his death as 'elf of Geirstad'. In the *Vita Anskarii*, the Swedish king Eirik is similarly worshipped as a god after his death with 'votive offerings and sacrifices' (ch.26). Perhaps the burial mound at Hørning described above was once the focus of a similar cult.

Memories of the dead remained important to those still living, and were included in religious practice. According to *Heimskringla*, at every sacrifice alongside toasts to the gods, everyone 'drank toasts for their relations who had been buried, and that was called 'Remembrance'' (*Hákonar saga Aðalsteinsfóstra*, ch.14).

BIBLIOGRAPHY

Ahlbäck, T. (ed.) (1990) *Old Norse and Finnish Religions and Cultic Place-Names*

Alkarp, M. & Price, N. (2005) 'Tempel av guld eller kyrka av trä? Markradarundersöhningar vid Gamla Uppsala kyrka' *Fornvännen* 100

Allen, W.E.D. (1960) 'The Poet and the Spae-Wife: an attempt to reconstruct Al-Ghazal's embassy to the Vikings' *Saga Book* 15

Ament, H. (1975) 'Merowingische Grabhügel' in Schlesinger 1975

Anderson, H., Carelli P. & Ersgard, L. (eds) (1997) *Visions of the Past: Trends and Traditions in Swedish Medieval Archaeology, Lund studies in medieval archaeology* 1

Anderson, W.B. (1965) *The poems and Letters of Sidonius*

Andrén, A. (1993) 'Doors to Other Worlds: Scandinavian Death Rituals' *Journal of European Archaeology* vol.1

Arnold, B. (1996) ' 'Honorary males' or women of substance? Gender, status and power in Iron Age Europe' *Journal of European Archaeology* 3(2)

Arrhenius, B. (1983) 'The chronology of the Vendel graves' in Lamm and Nordström 1983

Artelius, T. (2000) *Bortglömda föreställningar. Begravningsritual och begravningsplats i halländsk yngre järnalder*

Badou, E. (1989) 'Hög – gård – helgedom i Mellannorrland under den äldre järnåldern' *Arkeologi I norr* 2

Baetke, W. (1973) *Kleine Schriften: Geschichte, Recht und Religion in germanischem Schrifttum.* Ed. Kurt Rudolph & Ernst Walter

Barnes, G. & Clunies Ross, M. (2000) *Old Norse Myths, Literature and Society: Proceedings of the 11th International Saga Conference*

Battista, S. (2000) 'Interpretations of the Roman Pantheon in the Old Norse Hagiographic Sagas' in Barnes & Clunies Ross 2000

Bersu, G. & Wilson, D.M. (1966) *Three Viking Graves in the Isle of Man, The Society for Medieval Archaeology Monograph Series* 1

Blair, J. (1995) 'Anglo-Saxon Pagan Shrines and their Prototypes' *ASSAH* 8

Bauchhenss, G. & Nölke, P. (1981) *Die Iupitersäulen in den germanischen Provinzen*

Branston, B. (1957) *The Lost Gods of England*

Breeze, A. (1998) 'The Irish Nickname of Sitric Caoch (d.927) of York' *Saga Book* 25 pt.1

Briggs, C.S. (1995) 'Did They Fall Or Were They Pushed? Some Unresolved Questions About Bog Bodies' in Turner & Scaife 1995

Brink, S. (1996) 'Forsaringen – Nordens äldsta lagbud', in Roesdahl, E. & Meulengraht Sørensen, P. *Beretning fra femtende tværfaglige vikingesymposium,* Reports from the 15th interdisciplinary Viking symposium

Brink, S. (1990) 'Cult sites in northern Sweden' in Ahlbäck 1990

Brink, S. (1996) 'Political and Social Structures in Early Scandinavia: A Settlement-historical Pre-study of the Central Place' *Tor* 28

Brink, S. (2001) 'Mythologizing Landscape. Place and Space of Cult and Myth' in Hultgård 2001

Brink, S. (2002) 'Law and Legal Customs in Viking Age Scandinavia' in Jesch 2002

Brøndsted, Johannes 1960, 1965 *The Vikings*

Bruce-Miford, R. (1978) *The Sutton Hoo Ship Burial, II. Arms, Armour and Regalia*

Buchholz, P. (1969) 'Perspectives for Historical Research in Germanic Religion' *History of Religions* 8 (1968-9)

Buchholz, P. (1972) 'The Religious Geography of Pagan Scandinavia' *Mediaeval Scandinavia* 5

Buchholz, P. (1971) 'Shamanism - the Testimony of Old Icelandic Literary Tradition' *Mediaeval Scandinavia* 4

Buckland, T. (1980) 'The reindeer antlers of the Abbots Bromley Horn Dance: A re-examination' *Lore & Language* 3 (2)

Byock, J. (2001) *Viking Age Iceland*

Cawte, Dr E.C. (1978) *Ritual Animal Disguise: A Historical and Geographical Study of Animal Disguise in the British Isles*

Chaney, W.A. (1970) *The Cult of Kingship in Anglo-Saxon England: The transition from paganism to Christianity*

Christensen, A.E. (1975) 'The Jelling Monuments' *Mediaeval Scandinavia* 8

Christensen, T. (1982) 'Gerdrup-graven' *Årbog for Roskilde Museum* 2

Crumlin Pedersen, O. (1995) 'Boat Burials at Slusegaard and the Interpretation of the Boat-grave Custom' in Crumlin Pedersen & Munch Thye 1995

Crumlin Pedersen, O. & Munch Thye, B. (eds) (1995) *The Ship as Symbol in prehistoric and medieval Scandinavia*

Damico, H. (1990) 'The valkyrie reflex in Old English literature' in Damico & Olsen 1990

Damico, H. & Olsen, A.H. (eds) (1990) *New Readings on Women in Old English Literature*

Danielsson, I.M.B. (2001) 'Hemdrup-staven - ett nytt tolkningsförslag' *Fornvännen* 96

Davidson, T. (1959) 'Plough Rituals in England and Scotland' *The Agricultural History Review* VII

Davies, A. (1989) 'Witches in Anglo-Saxon England: Five Case Histories' in Scragg 1989

de Vries, J. (1952) 'La Valeur religieuse du mot germanique *irmin*' *Cahiers du Sud* 314

Dillmann, F.X. (1997) 'Kring de rituella gästebuden i fornskandinavisk religion' in Hultgård 1997

Dronke, U. (1996) *Myth and Fiction in early Norse Lands*

Dryden, J. (1683-6, revised by Arthur Hugh Clough 1864) *The Lives of the Noble Grecians and Romans*

DuBois, T.A. (1999) *Nordic Religions in the Viking Age*

Dumézil, G. (1973) (trans. F.R. Schröder) *The Gods of the Ancient Northmen*

Edsman, C.M. (1990) 'Opening Address' in Ahlbäck 1990

Ellis, H. (1943) *The Road to Hel*

Ellis Davidson, H.R. (1969, 1982) *Viking and Norse Mythology*

Ellis Davidson, H.R. (1998) *Roles of the Northern Goddess*

Ellis Davidson, H.R. (1964) *Gods and Myths of Northern Europe*

Ellis Davidson, H.R. (1976) *The Viking Road to Byzantium*

Ellis Davidson, H.R. (1989) *Myths and Symbols of Pagan Europe*

Ellis Davidson, H.R. (1993) *The Lost Beliefs of Northern Europe*

Elsner, H.(*c*.1989) *Wikinger Museum Haithabu: Schaufenster einer frühen Stadt*

Engdahl, K. & Kaliff, A. (eds) (1996) *Religion från stenålder till medeltid : artiklar baserade på Religionsarkeologiska nätverksgruppens konferens på Lövstadbruk den 1-3 december 1995*

Ewing, T. (1995) 'The Birth of Lugh – Óðinn and Loki among the Celts' *Sinsear* 8

(a version of this article is available online at www.historicalarts.co.uk/articles/sinsear/the_birth_of_lugh.html)

Ewing, T. (2003) 'Understanding the Heysham Hogback: a tenth-century sculpted stone monument and its context' *Transactions of the Historic Society of Lancashire and Cheshire*, Vol.152

Ewing, T. (2006) *Viking Clothing*

Falk, H. (1924) *Odensheite*

Faulkes, A. (1993) 'The sources of Skáldskaparmál: Snorri's intellectual background' in Wolf 1993

Foote, P. & Wilson, D.M. (1970) *The Viking Achievement*

Foote, P., Pálsson H. & Slay D. (eds) (1971) *Proceedings of the First International Saga Conference*

Freke, D. (1987) 'Pagan lady of Peel' *Archaeology today* 8/1 (February 1987)

Furuta, N. (2002) 'Fate in the *Íslendingasögur*, the *Poetic Edda* and *Beowulf* *Asterisk* XI.1

Gelling, P. & Ellis Davidson, H. (1969) *The Chariot of the Sun*

Glob, P.V. (1969) *The Bog People*

Göransson, E.M. (1999) *Bildor av kvinnor och kvinnlighet: genus och kroppsspråk under övergången till kristendomen*

Görman, M. (1990) 'Nordic and Celtic' in Ahlbäck 1990

Gräslund, A.S. (1967) 'Ett forhistoriskt brödfynd från Östergötland' *Fornvännen* 62

Gräslund, A.S. (1969) 'Särdag inom vikingatidens gravskick' *Nordsvensk forntid*

Gräslund, A.S. (2001) 'Living with the Dead. Reflections on Food Offerings in Graves' in Hultgård 2001

Grässlund, A.S. (1980) *The Burial Customs: A Study of the Graves on Björkö (Birka IV)*

Green, D.H. (1998) *Language and History in the early Germanic world*

Green, D.H. and Siegmund, F. (2003) *The continental Saxons from the migration period to the tenth century: an ethnographic perspective*

Green, M.A. (1992) *Symbol and Image in Celtic Religious Art*

Green, M.A. (1998) 'Humans as Ritual Victims in the later prehistory of western Europe' *Oxford Journal of Archaeology*

Green, M.A. (2004) 'Women and Goddesses in the Celtic World' in Sutcliffe 2004

Green, M.A. (2001) *Dying for the Gods*

Griffiths, B. 1996 (2003) *Aspects of Anglo-Saxon Magic*

Grimm, J. (1880-88) *Teutonic Mythology*

Gunnell, T. (1995) *The Origins of Drama in Scandinavia*

Gunnell, T. (2006) 'How elvish were the *Álfar*?' in McKinnell & Kick 2006

Hägg, I. (1984) *Die Textilfunde aus dem Hafen von Haithabu*

Hall, A. (2007) *Elves in Anglo-Saxon England: Matters of Belief, Health, Gender and Identity*

Hallberg, P. (1971) 'The Concept of Gipta-Gæfa-Hamingja in Old Norse Literature', in Foote *et al.*

Heather, P. (1999) *The Visigoths from the migration period to the seventh century: an ethnographic perspective*

Henriksen, V. (1970) *Christmas in Norway Past and Present*

Herschend, F. (1993) 'The origin of the hall in southern Scandinavia' *Tor* 25

Herschend, F. (2003) 'Material Metaphors: Some Late Iron and Viking Age Examples' in Ross & Barnes 2003

Hines, J. (2000) 'Myth and Reality: the Contribution of Archaeology' in Barnes & Clunies Ross 2000

Hines, J. (2002) 'The Conversion of the Old Saxons' in Green & Siegmund 2003

Hnefill Aðalsteinsson J. (1999) 'Religious Ideas in *Sonatorrek*' *Saga Book* 25

Hnefill Aðalsteinsson J. (1985) 'Blót and Þing: The Function of the Tenth Century Goði' *Temenos* 21

Holmqvist, W. (1960) 'The Dancing Gods' *Acta Archaeologica* 31

Holmqvist, W. (1960) 'The Dancing Gods' *Acta Archaeologica* 31

Holtzmann, R. (ed.) (1935) *Die Chronik des Bischofs Thietmar von Merseburg*

Hultgård, A. (ed. Stausberg, M., Sundqvist, O. & van Nahl, A.) (2001) *Kontinuität und Brüche in der Religionsgeschichte. Festschrift für Anders Hultgård zu seinem 65. Geburtstag am 23.12. 2001*

Hultgård, A. (1997) *Uppsalakulten och Adam av Bremen, Religionshistoriska forskningsrapporter från Uppsala*; 11, in Trøndelag *Norwegian Archaeological Review* 2

Ingstad, A.S. (1995) 'The Interpretation of the Oseberg-find' in Crumlin Pedersen & Munch Thye 1995

Jansson, S.B.F. (1962) *The Runes of Sweden* (revised and reissued as *Runes in Sweden* 1987)

Jesch, J. 1991 *Women in the Viking Age*

Jesch, J. (ed.) (2002) *The Scandinavians from the Vendel Period to the Tenth Century: An Ethnographic Perspective*

Johansen, Ø. (1982) 'En dobbeltgrav fra vikingtid i et "funnfattig" område' *Viking* 45 (1981)

Steffensen, J. (1968) 'Aspects of life in Iceland in the heathen period' *Saga Book* 17

Jones, G. (1968, 1973) *A History of the Vikings*

Kabell, A. (1980) *Skalden und Schamanen*

Kaul, F. (1991) *Gundestrupkedelen*

Kiil, V. (1962) 'The Norse prophetess and the ritually induced prostitution' *Norveg* 9

King, P.D. (1987) *Charlemagne: translated sources*

Kokowski, A. (1995) *Schätze der Ostgoten*

Kokowski, A. (2007) *Goci. Od Skandzy do Campi Gothorum*

Koktvergaard Zeiten, M. (1997) 'Amulets and amulet use in Viking Age Denmark' *Acta Archaeologica* 68

Krusch, B. (ed.) (1885) *Liber in Gloria Confessorum*, Gregory of Tours in *Monumenta Germaniae Historica, Scriptores Rerum Merovingicarum* 1, 2

Kurze, F. (ed.) (1895) *Annales regni Francorum*

Lambrechts, P. (1942) *Contibutions a l'Études des Divinités Celtiques*

Lamm, J.P. & H.-Å. Nordström (eds) (1983) *Vendel Period Studies. Transactions of the Boat-grave symposium in Stockholm, February 2-3, 1981*

Larsson, L. & Hårdh, B. (eds.) (1998) *Centrala platser, centrala frågor: samhällsstrukturen under järnåldern: en vänbok till Berta Stjernquist*

Larsson, L. (ed.) (2004) *Continuity for centuries: a ceremonial building and its context at Uppåkra, southern Sweden*

Levison, W. (ed.) (1913) *Vita Wilfridi I. episcopi Eboracensis*, Eddius Stephanus in *Monumenta Germaniae Historica, Scriptores Rerum Merovingiearum* 6

Lidén, H.E. (1969) 'From Pagan Sanctuary to Christian Church. The Excavation of Mære Church in Trøndelag' *Norwegian Archaeological Review* 2

Lindow, J. (ed.) (1986) *Structure and Meaning in Old Norse Literature: New Approaches to Textual Analysis and Literary Criticism*

Lindqvist, S. (1923) 'Hednatemplet i Uppsala' *Fornvännen* 18

Lindqvist, S. (1964) 'Forngutniska altaren och därtill knuta studier' *Kungliga humanistiska vetnskaps-samfundet i Uppsala. Årsbok 1960-2*

Lindqvist, S. (1967) 'Uppsala hednatempel och första katedral. Gammal stridsfåga i nytt ljus' *Nordisk Tidskrift* 42

Ljungkvist, J. (2005) 'Uppsala högars datering och några konsekvenser av en omdatering till tidiga vendeltiden' *Fornvännen* 100

Lönnroth, L. (1986) 'Dómaldi's Death and the Myth of Sacral Kingship' in Lindow 1986

Lönnroth, L. (1986) 'Dómaldi's Death and the Myth of Sacral Kingship' in *Structure and Meaning in Old Norse Literature: New Approaches to Textual Analysis and Literary Criticism* John Lindow *et al.* (ed.)

Lucy, S. (2000) *Anglo-Saxon Way of Death: Burial rites in early England*

MacCulloch, J.A. (1930) *Eddic Mythology* (Volume II of 13 volumes *The Mythology of All Races*, ed. John Arnott MacCulloch)

Magnusson, M. (1976) *Hammer of the North*

Malinowski, B. (1948) *Magic, Science and Religion*

Mauss, M. 1925, (1967) *The Gift*

McKinnell, J.S. & Ruggerini, M.E. (1994) *Both One and Many: Essays on Change and Variety in Late Norse Heathenism*

McKinnell, J.S. (2000) 'Encounters with *Völur*' in Barnes & Clunies Ross 2000

McKinnell, J.S. (2005) *Meeting the Other in Norse Myth and Legend*

McKinnell, J.S. & Kick, D. (2006) *The Fantastic in Old Norse-Icelandic Literature / Sagas and the British Isles: Preprint papers of the 13th International Saga Conference*

McTurk, R.W. (1974) 'Sacral Kingship in Ancient Scandinavia: A Review of Some Recent Writings' *Saga Book* 19

McTurk, R.W. (1993) 'Kingship' in Pulsiano *et al.* 1993

McTurk, R.W. (1994) 'Scandinavian sacral kingship revisited' *Saga Book* 24

Meaney, A.L. (1964) *A Gazeteer of Early Anglo-Saxon Burial Sites*

Meaney, A.L. (1981) *Anglo-Saxon Amulets and Curing Stones*

Meaney, A.L. (1995) 'Pagan English Sanctuaries, Place-Names and Hundred Meeting-Places' *ASSAH* 8

Miller, S. (ed.) (2001) *Charters of the New Minster, Winchester*, Anglo-Saxon Charters 9

Moisl, H. (1981) 'Anglo-Saxon royal genealogies and Germanic oral tradition' *Journal of Medieval History* 7:3

Montgomery, J.E. (2000) 'Ibn Fadlan and the Rusiyyah' *Journal of Arabic and Islamic Studies* 3

Montgomery, J.E. (2001) 'Ibn Rusta's Lack of 'Eloquence', the Rus and Samanid Cosmography' *Edebiyat* 12

Mortensen, P. & R., Birgit M. (eds) (1991) *Fra Stamme til Stat I Danmark 2: Høvdingesamfund og kongemagt*

Motz, L. (1984) 'Gods and Demons of the Wilderness. A study in Norse tradition' *Arkiv för Nordisk Filologi*

Motz, L. (1984) 'The Winter Goddess: Percht, Holda and Related Figures' *Folklore* 95:2

Müller-Wille, M. (1993) 'Burial Mounds and Burial Practices' in Pulsiano *et al.* 1993

Müller-Wille, M. (1993) 'Graves' in Pulsiano *et al.* 1993

Munksgaard, E.(1970) *Denmark: An Archaeological Guide*

Murray, A.C. (ed.) (1998) *After Rome's Fall: Narrators and Sources of Early Medieval History*

Murray, A.C. (1998) '*Post vocantur Merohingii*: Fredegar, Merovech, and 'Sacral Kingship" in Murray 1998

Niebuhr, B.G. (ed.) (1838-9) *Compendium Historiarum (Ioannis Scylitzae ope)* 2 vols. Cedrenus, Georgius

Nielsen, A.L. (1997) 'Pagan cultic and votive acts at Borg' in Andersen *et al.* 1997

Nilsson, B.E. (1976) 'The Runic 'Fish-Amulet' from Öland: A Solution' *Mediaeval Scandinavia* 9

Nordahl, E. (1996) *Templum quod Ubsola dicitur ... i arkeologisk belysning*

Nordberg, A. (2002) 'Vertikalt placerade vapen i vikingatida gravar' *Fornvännen* 97

Nørlund, P. (1948) *Trelleborg*

North, R. (1991) *Pagan words and Christian meanings*

North, R. (1997) *Heathen gods in Old English Literature*

North, R. (2000) '*goð geyja*: the limits of humour in Old Norse-Icelandic paganism' in Barnes & Clunies Ross 2000

Olsen, M. (1915) *Hedenske kultminder i norske stedsnavne* 1

Olsen, M. (1928) *Farms and Fanes of Ancient Norway: The Place-Names of a Country Discussed in their Bearings on Social and Religious History*

Olsen, O. (1966) *Hørg, hof og kirke*

Oosten, J.G. (1985) *The war of the gods*

Owen, G.R. (1981) *Rites and Religions of the Anglo-Saxons*

Perkins, R. (2001) *Thor the Wind Raiser and the Eyrarland Image*

Phillpotts, B.S. (1913) 'Temple Administration and Chieftainship in pre-Christian Norway and Iceland' *Saga Book* 8

Pluskowski, A. (2000) 'The Sacred Gallows: Sacrificial Gallows to Óðinn' *Archaeological Review from Cambridge* 17/2

Pope, J.A. (ed.) (1967-8) *Homilies of Ælfric: a Supplementary Collection* EETS

Price, N. (2002) *The Viking way*

Pulsiano, P., Wolf, K. Acker P. & Fry D.K. (eds.) 1993 *Medieval Scandinavia: An Encyclopedia*

Raith, J. (ed.) (1964, 2nd ed.) *Die altenglische Version des Haltigar'schen Bussbuches* Bibliothek der angelsächsischen Prosa 13 (Darmstadt)

Ramskou, T. (1965) 'Vikingerne ofrede mennesker' *Nationalmuseets arbejdsmark* 1963-5

Randsborg, K. (1980) *The Viking Age in Denmark: The formation of a state*

Randsborg, K. (1995) *Hjortspring: Warfare and Sacrifice in Early Europe*

Reichert, H. (1991-3) 'Gutani ? Wi Hailag' *Die Sprache* 35

Reynolds, A.J. (1996) 'Anglo-Saxon human sacrifice at Cuddesdon and Sutton Hoo?' *Papers from the Institute of Archaeology* 7

Richards, J.D. (1991, 2004) *Viking Age England*

Richards, J.D., Marcus Jecock, Lizzie Richmond and Catherine Tuck (1995) 'The Viking barrow cemetery at Heath Wood, Ingleby, Derbyshire' *Medieval Archaeology* 39

Riisøy, A.I. (2005) 'From law to list' *Bulletin of Medieval Canon Law, New Series* Vol. 26

Rives, J.B. (trans.) (1999) *Tacitus: Germania*

Roesdahl, E. (1987) *The Vikings*

Roesdahl, E. (1982) *Viking Age Denmark*

Roscoe, W. (1996) 'Priests of the Goddess: Gender transgression in ancient religion' *History of Religions* 35

Ross, M.C. & Barnes, G. (2003) *Old Norse Myths, Literature and Society* van der Sanden, W.A.B. (1995) 'Bog Bodies on the Continent: Developments since 1965, with Special Reference to the Netherlands' in Turner & Scaife 1995

Saupe, H.A. (ed.) (1891) *Der Indiculus superstitionum et paganiarum, ein Verzeichnis heidnischer und abergläubischer Gebräuche und Meinungen aus der Zeit Karls des Grossen*

Schlesinger, W. (ed.) (1975) *Althessen im Frankenreich*

Schmidt, Holger (1994) *Building Customs in Viking Age Denmark*

von Schnurbein, S. (2003) 'Shamanism in the Old Norse tradition: A theory between ideological camps' *History of Religions* 43

Schönbäck, B. (1980) 'Båtgravskicket' in Sandwall, A. (ed.) *Vendeltid*

Schönbäck, B. (1983) 'The custom of burials in boats' in Lamm & Nordström 1983

Schönbäck, B. (1983) 'The custom of burials in boats' *Vendel Period Studies. Transactions of the Boat-grave symposium in Stockholm, February 2-3, 1981*

Schwarcz, A. (1999) 'Cult and Religion among the Tervingi and the Visigoths and their Conversion to Christianity' in Heather 1999

Scragg, D.G. (ed.) (1989) *Superstition and popular Medicine in Anglo-Saxon England*

Simpson, J. (1967) *Everyday Life in the Viking Age*

Skre, D. & Stylegar, F.A. 2004 *Kaupang: The Viking Town*

Solberg, B. (1999) '"Holy white stones". Remains of fertility cult in Norway' in *Völker an Nord- und Ostsee und die Franken.* von Freeden, Uta & Koch, Ursula (ed.)1999

Sørensen, P.M. (1983) *The Unmanly Man: Concepts of Sexual Defamation in Early Northern Society* (trans. Joan Turville-Petre)

Sørensen, P.M. (1991) 'Håkon den Gode og guderne. Nogle bemærkninger om religion og centralmagt I det tiende århundrede – og om religion og kildekritik' in Mortensen & Rasmussen 1991

Speidel, M.P. (2002) 'Berserks: A History of Indo-European 'Mad Warriors'' *Journal of World History*

Speidel, M.P. (2004) *Ancient Germanic Warriors: Warrior Styles from Trajan's Column to Icelandic Sagas*

Spickermann, W., Cancik, H. & Rüpke, J. (eds) (2001) *Religion in den germanischen Provinzen Roms*

Stanley, E.G. (1975, 2000) *The Search for Anglo-Saxon Paganism* (reprinted in *Imagining the Anglo-Saxon Past* 2000)

Steinsland, G. (ed.) (1986a) *Words and Objects: towards a dialogue between archaeology and history of religion*

Stenberger, M. (1956) 'Tuna in Badelunda: a grave in central Sweden with Roman vessels' *Acta archaeologica* 27

Storm, G. (1885) *Norges gamle Love* IV

Ström, Å.V. (1990) 'Personal Piety in Nordic Heathenism' in Ahlbäck 1990

Strömbäck, D. (1935) *Sejd - Textstudier i nordisk religionshistoria*

Sundqvist, O. (2002) *Freyr's Offspring: rulers and religion in ancient Svea society*

Sutcliffe, S.J. (2004) *Religion: Empirical Studies*

Swanson, G.E. (1960) *The Birth of the Gods* Michigan

Thorpe, B. (1840) *Ancient Laws and Institutes*

Todd, M. (1972) *Everyday Life of the Barbarians: Goths, Franks and Vandals*

Todd, M. (1975) *The Northern Barbarians: 100BC – AD300*

Todd, M. (2004) *The early Germans*

Turner, R.C. & Scaife, R.G. (ed.) (1995) *Bog Bodies: New Discoveries and New Perspectives*

Turville-Petre, E.O.G. (1935) *The Cult of Frey in the Evening of Paganism*

Turville-Petre, E.O.G. (1964) *Myth and Religion of the North*

Van der Sanden, W.A.B. (1995) 'Bog-Bodies on the Continent: Developments since 1965, with Special Reference to the Netherlands' in Turner & Scaife 1995

Van der Sanden, W.A.B. (1996) *Through Nature to Eternity: The bog bodies of northwest Europe*

Wallace-Hadrill, J.M. (1971) *Early Germanic Kingship in England and on the Continent*

Warner, D.A. (trans.) (2001) *Thietmar's 'Chronicon'* MUP

Watson, J. (2005) 'Laid to rest – two Anglo-Saxon graves reconstructed' *Research News* 2 (Newsletter of the English Heritage Research Department)

Welch, M. (1992) *Anglo-Saxon England*

Wilson, D. (1985) 'A Note on OE *hearg* and *weoh* as Place-Name elements Representing Different Types of Pagan Saxon Worship Sites' *ASSAH* 4

Wilson, D. (1992) *Anglo-Saxon Paganism*

Wolf, A. (publisher) (1993) *Snorri Sturluson. Kolloquium anläßlich der 750*

Woolf, G. (2001) 'Representation as Cult: the case of the Jupiter columns', in Spickermann *et al.* 2001

INDEX

Italicised entries relate to images

Abbots Bromley (Staffordshire, England) 36
Adam of Bremen, *Gesta Hammaburgensis* 15, 16, 19, 24, 42, 44, 47, 60-2, 64, 68, 69, 74, 79
Ælfric, *De falsis diis* 47
ælf-sīden 85, 115
Æsir 54, 65, 84, 113, 115, 116, 121-3; see also 'Odin', 'Thor'
Al Istakhri 138, 139
Al Mas'udi 138, 139
Alcuin, *Vita Willibrordi* 23, 46
Althing 76, 77, 111
al-Turtushi, Ibrahim 25, 69
Alvheim (Bohuslän, Sweden) 115
Angel of Death (*malak al-mawt*) 108
Anglo-Saxon Chronicle 32
Annals of the Four Masters 32
Annals of the Frankish Kings 28
Ansgar, see *Vita Anskarii*
Apple Down (West Sussex, England) 133
Ash (Kent, England) 58, *29*
Atlakviða 32, 33
Aurinia 73
Austrfaravísur 62, 115
Avaldsnes (Karmøy, Rogaland, Norway) 140

Bække (Jylland, Denmark) 134, 135
Baldrs draumar 143
Baldursheimur (Suður-Þingeyjarsýsla, Iceland), possible idol from, 55
Balladoole (Isle of Man) 135, 136
Ballateare (Isle of Man) 135, 139
Bällsta (Uppland, Sweden) 134
bautasteiner 135
bed burial 131
Bede, *De Temporum Ratione* 42, 105
Bede, *Historia Ecclesiastica* 24, 52, 54, 61, 65, 67, 68, 95-6, 97
Beowulf 27, 33, 63, 136, 142, 149
Bergen (Sogn og Fjordane, Norway) 34
julebukk ceremony 39, 41, 43
Berne Scholia 19
berserks 118-121
Birka (Mälaren, Sweden 58, 73, 128, 131, 132, 133, 137, 138, 140, 141, 142, 144
boat burial, see 'ship burial'
bog sacrifice and burial 18-19, 21, 22, 23, 26-8, 50, 53, 67, 68, 74, *5*, *6*, *20*, *21*, *34*
Boniface, see Willibald
Borg (Lofoten, Norway) 63, 66
Borg (Östergötland, Sweden) 66
Borremose (Jylland, Denmark) 19
Bosa saga 33
Braak (Holstein, Germany) 51, 52
Brink, Stefan 71
Broddenbjerg (Jylland, Denmark) 51, 67, *20*
Buckland (Kent, England) 136
Burchard of Worms, *Decretum* 102, 104, 108, 117
Buslubæn 33

Caesar, *De Bello Gallico* 23, 27, 66, 71, 100
Canons of Edgar 34
Capitulatio de partibus saxoniae 44
Castledyke (Humberside, England) 128
chamber graves 131, 133, 140, 142, 143, *47*
Charles the Great, emperor 50, 68
Charlevanne (Paris, France) 27
Chernaia Mogila (Chernigov, Ukraine) possible idol from, 55, *24*
Clontarf (Dublin, Ireland) 101
Codex Abrogans 69

Codex Regius 88, 142, 143; see also individual named poems
Cogadh Gaedhel re Gallaibh 70, 72
Coifi 52, 96, 97
Constantine Porphyrogenitus, *De Administrando Imperio* 24, 28, 46
Constantine Porphyrogenitus, *De cerimoniis aulae Byzantiae* 36
cremation 19, 58, 127-8, 132, 133, 135, 136, 138-9, 140-1, 143, 144, 145

Darraðarljóð 101, 108, 117
Dätgen (Schleswig Holstein, Germany) 19
Dejbjerg (Jylland, Denmark) 53, *21*
Díar 121-2
Dio Cassius, *Historia Romana* 73
Diplomatorium Norvegicum 41
dísa-blót 105, 116, 118
Discipulus Umbrensium 83, 87
Dudo of St Quentin 19

Egils saga 30, 33, 47, 68, 69, 74, 76, 100, 119, 120, 134
Eiríks saga rauða 30, 84
Ejsbøl (Jylland, Denmark) 26, 74, *34*
Ekhammar (Östergötland, Sweden) *39*
Eligius, see *Vita Eligii*
elves 85, 112, 115, 116, 146
Encomium Emmae 117
Eresburg (now Obermarsburg, Westfalen, Germany) 50
ergi 87, 96, 107, 111
Eyrarland (Eyjafjörður, Iceland) possible idol from, 55, *25*
Eyrbyggja saga 19, 21, 31, 34, 61, 64, 70, 72, 77, 134

Fafnismál 103
Feddet (Sjælland, Denmark) possible idol from, 55
Flateyjarbók 59, 60, 61, 63, 79, 86, 103, 139, 144, 146
Fønsskov (Fyn, Denmark) Thor's hammer from, *28*
food and drink, feasts 24, 25, 26, 27, 28, 32, 42, 43, 45, 60, 62-4, 65, 66, 70, 74, 78, 80, 84, 88, 91, 115, 117, 125, 131, 137-8, 144-5, 146
Forlev Nymølle (Jylland, Denmark) 2 8
Forsa (Hälsingland, Sweden) 71-2, 77, *33*
Fosite 23, 46
Fóstbræðra saga 89
Foulden (Norfolk, England) 138
Franks Casket *15*, (*16*)
Frayre de Joy e Sor de Placer 103
Frey 18, 24, 25, 29, 32, 34, 43, 46, 52, 53, 54, 55, 58, 110, 113, 114, 115, 116, 117, 121, 122, *26*
Freyja 22, 52, 67, 73, 84, 88, 102, 110, 111, 112, 113, 116, 121, 123,
Friðþjófs saga 54
Frösö (Jämtland, Sweden) 46, 48, 114, 143
Frostathing, *Frostaþings lag* 68, 73, 77
Fyrkat (Jylland, Denmark) 142, 143

Gaesmere, Jove's Oak 46, 48, 143
Gallehus (Slesvig, Denmark) golden horns from 36, *12*
Ganna 73
Gaular (Sogn og Fjordane, Norway) 74
Gautreks saga 17, 23, 144
Gesta Herewardi 100-1
Gilton (Kent, England) 58
Gísla saga 34, 87, 120, 144
Glavendrup (Fyn, Denmark) 69, 134, 140
goði 64, 69, 72, 73, 76, 97, 116, 121-2
Gokstad (Vestfold, Norway) 133, 138, 141
Goodmanham (Yorkshire, England) 67, 68, 97, 132
Gørlev (Sjælland, Denmark) 134
Gothikon 39
Grágás 120
grave goods 35, 53, 117, 131, 132, 136-8, 142, 143, 144, *48*
Gregory I 'the Great', Pope 24, 61, 65
Dialogues 42
Gregory II, Pope 23
Gregory of Tours, *Liber in Gloria Confessorum* 53
Gregory of Tours, *Vita S. Galli* (*Vita Patriae*) 65
Grettis saga 120
Grímnismál 66, 92, 93, 102, 115, 120, 126
Grógaldr 143
Grottasöngr 74
Grýla, guising character 39
Gudhjem (Bornholm, Denmark) 49
Guðrúnarkviða I 115
Gulathing 66, 76, 77, 79
Guldgubber 55, 58, 66, *22*
Gunderup (Jylland, Denmark) 134, 140
Gunnars þáttr helmings 52, 73
Gunnell, Terry 35, 39
Guta saga 24, 67, 78
Gutalög 24, 67
Gutenstein (Baden-Württemberg, Germany) *14*
Guthlac, see *Vita Guthlaci*
gyðja 72, 73, 109, 121

Hærvejen 135
Hákonar saga Aðalsteinsfóstra 25, 35, 62, 63, 70, 74, 146
Hallfreðar saga Vandræðaskalds 55
Haltigar, *Penitential* 44
Hamðismál 115

Haralds saga Harðráða 102
Haralds saga ins hárfagra 87, 116, 117, 124
Haraldskvæði 34, 107, 118,
Hárbarðslóð 48, 111
Harreby (Jylland, Denmark) 135
Harrow-on-the-Hill (Middlesex, England) 65, 67
Hauks þáttr hábrókar 34, 52
Hauksbók 28, 47, 70, 78
Haustlöng 115
Hávamál 17, 29, 32, 34, 51, 52, 88-91, 92, 93, 95, 96, 97, 101, 111, 112, 135, 144; *Gesta þáttr* 89
hearg 65, 67
Hedeby (or Haithabu, in the modern district of Haddeby, Schleswig-Holstein, Germany) 25, 36, 137, 141, *8*
Heimlysing 60
Heimskringla 24, 25, 74, 146
Helgakviða Hiorvardssonar 108
Helgakviða Hundingsbana I 103, 106, 108
Helgakviða Hundingsbana II 101, 103
Helligkvinde (Bornholm, Denmark) 49
Helreið Brynhildar 143
Hervarar saga ok Heiðreks 24
Hestehagen (Østfold, Norway) 140
Hestestenene (Bornholm, Denmark) 49
Historia Norwegiae 116
hof 25, 62, 64, 66, 67, 68, 122, *32*
Hofstaðir (Mývatn, Iceland) 63, 64
Hög (Hälsingland, Sweden) 71
Högom (Medelpad, Sweden) 63
hörgr 66, 67
Hørning (Jylland, Denmark) 143, 146
horses 24, 26, 27, 34-5, 41, 49, 69, 95, 96, 138, 145, *7*
Housesteads (Northumberland, England) 76
Hrafnsmál, see *Haraldskvæði*
Hrólfs saga kraka 84, 92, 101, 103, 112, 115, 116, 119, 120
Hundabrævið 68
Hundorp (Gudbrandsdalen, Norway) 60
Huseby (Vestfold, Norway) 62, 63
Hyndluljóð 67, 110, 111, 112

Ibn Fadlan, *Kitāb ilā Malik al-Saqāliba* 24, 28, 29, 30, 52, 69, 108, 133, 138, 139, 152
Ibn Rusta, *Kitab al-A'laq al-nafisa* 21, 97, 131
idisi 101, 115
idols 29, 30, 33, 46, 47, 50-60, 61, 62, 64, 65, 67, 68, 73, 92, 93, 123, *15*, *20*, (*21*), *23*, *24*, *25*, *26*, *27*, *31*, (*32*)
Île de Groix (Bretagne, France) 141
Illerup (Jylland, Denmark) 26
Indiculus Superstitionem et Paganiarum 19, 44, 46, 53, 54, 66, 145
Ingleby (Derbyshire, England) 133, 141
inhumation 127-8, 132, 133, 136, 138, 140, 141, 142

Irminsul 28, 50
Isidore of Seville, *Etymologiae* 60

Järrestad (Skåne, Sweden) 66
Jelling (Jylland, Denmark) 48, 49, 63, 133, 135
Jómsvikinga saga 32, 101, 108, 117, 118
Jordanes, *Getica* 18
julebukk 39, 41, 42, 43
Jupiter pillars (*Jupitersäulen*) 50
Jurby (Isle of Man) 144

Källby (Västergötland, Sweden) *9*
Käringsjön (Stockholm, Sweden) 28
Kayhausen (Niedersachsen, Germany) 19, 23
Kiil, Vilhelm 111
Kjalnesinga saga 19
Klinta (Öland, Sweden) 144
Köln (Nordrhein-Westfalen, Germany) 65, 105, 106
Kolsundet (Södermanland, Sweden) 134
Köstrup (Fyn, Denmark) 140
Kragehul (Fyn, Denmark) 26
Kristni saga 21, 23, 47, 70, 72
Kvalsund (Finnmark, Norway) 26
Kvasir 121, 122
Kvinneby (Öland, Sweden), amulet from, 34

Ladby (Fyn, Denmark) 138, 141, 142
Lakenheath (Suffolk, England) 138
'Land remedy', Anglo-Saxon charm 28, 29, 31, 34, 54
Landnámabók 28, 31, 32, 47, 48, 55, 61, 72, 80, 101, 119, 120, 134, 139
Lapwing Hill (Derbyshire, England) 131
Lärbro Stora Hammars (Gotland, Sweden) *2*, (*15*)
Lärbro Tängelgårda (Gotland, Sweden) *49*, *50*
Laverstock (Wiltshire, England) 146
Laws of the Northumbrian Priests 67
Laxdæla saga 34, 86, 87, 88, 143, 145
Lebuin, see *Vita Lebuini*
Lejre (Sjælland, Denmark) 15, 17, 24, 63, 74, 134, 139, *32*
Lejre Chronicle 74
Leo Diaconus, *Historia* 120
Liber Pœnitentalis 31, 67
Liebenau (Niedersachsen, Germany) 132, 135
Lindby (Skåne, Sweden), possible idol from, 55, 93, *27*, *38*
Lindqvist, Sune 62
Liudger, see *Vita Liudgeri*
Ljunga (Skönberga, Sweden) 137
Lokasenna 88, 111, 113, 115
Loki 88, 111, 112, 149
Lund (Skåne, Sweden) possible idol from, 55, *23*
Lytir 52, 54, 117

Mære (Trøndelag, Norway) 59-60, 61, 63, 66
Masłomęcz (Lublin, Poland) 133
Matres, Matronae 105-7, 108, 40, 41, 42, (43)
McKinnell, John 86, 116
Meaney, Audrey 58, 102
Merseburg charms 101, 115
Mill Hill (Kent, England) 136
Mimir 93, 121, 122, 123
modraneht, see Bede, *De Temporum ratione*
mound burial 17, 46, 48, 53, 63, 74, 77, 117, 127, 131, 132-5, 136, 139, 140, 142, 143, 144, 146

Namdalen (Nord-Trøndelag, Norway) 133
Nebel (Schleswig Holstein, Germany) 58
Nerthus 22, 52, 53, 54, 110, 114, 117
Nettersheim (Nordrhein-Westfalen, Germany) 105, 108, *40*
'Nine Herbs Charm', Anglo-Saxon charm 95
Njáls saga 60, 61, 131
Njarðarlög, Tysnes 114
Njörd 25, 32, 66, 110, 113, 114, 116, 121, 122
Nornagests þáttr 86, 92, 103-4, 106, 108
Noyon (Picardie, France) 34
Nydam (Jylland, Denmark) 26, 28, 74, *34*

Oberdorla (Thüringen, Germany) 28, 50, 53, 60, 68
Oddrúnagrátr 107
Odin 17-8, 19, 23, 25, 32, 34, 47, 48, 50, 55, 74, 88, 90-1, 92-3, 95, 96, 98, 109, 110, 111, 112, 115, 116, 117, 119, 120, 121, 122, 123, 126, 136, 142, 143, 144, (2), *27*
Ólafs saga helga 30, 60, 61, 74, 76, 77, 79
Ólafs saga Tryggvasonar 24, 59, 60, 86, 87
Ólafs þáttr Geirstaðaálfs 146
Olaus Magnus, *Historia de gentibus* 35, *7*
Oldendorf (Niedersachsen, Germany) 133
Orkneyinga saga 88, 117
Orlunda (Östergötland, Sweden) 137
Orosius, *Historiæ* 27, 66
Örvar-Odds saga 28, 84, 86, 117
Oseberg (Vestfold, Norway), burial from, 53, 60, 117, 133, 139, 141, 142
Oseberg (Vestfold, Norway), headpost from, 60, *16*
Oseberg (Vestfold, Norway), tapestry from, 36, 109, 120, *3*, *10*, *11*, *43*
Ota 72, 117

Perceforest 103-4
pillars and poles, wooden 25, 28, 33, 39, 41, 42, 43, 47, 50, 64, 67-8, 133, 134
Pioneer Grave, Lakenheath (Suffolk, England) 138
Plutarch, *Caesar* 100
Portway, Andover (Hampshire, England) 135
Possendorf (Thüringen, Germany) 60
Price, Neil S. 58, 73, 93, 112, 144
Prittlewell (Essex, England) 131

Ræbild (Jylland, Denmark) 51
Ragnars saga loðbrókar 61
Raknehaugen (Akershus, Norway) 134
Rällinge (Södermanland, Sweden), idol from 55, *26*
Rappendam (Sjælland, Denmark) 28, 53
Reginsmál 92
Repton (Derbyshire, England) 58
Ribe (Jylland, Denmark) 93, *36*, (*37*)
Rígsþula 117
Rögubben (Östergötland, Sweden) 49, *19*
Rude Eskildstrup (Sjælland, Denmark) 60, *31*
Rus 21, 24, 25, 28, 29, 30, 36, 46, 52, 97, 108, 120, 134, 136, 138, 139, 140, 145

Sancton (East Yorkshire, England) 132, 138
Sanda (Uppland, Sweden) 66
Saxo, *Gesta Danorum* 18, 24, 42, 74, 92, 96, 98, 99, 100, 101, 104, 107
Seiðr 72-3, 84-8, 91, 96, 101, 107, 110-2, 113, 114, 115, 116, 120, 121, 122, 124, 125
Semnones, holy grove of 16, 17, 30, 45, 74, 76, 78
Sermo lupi, see Wulfstan
Setesdal (Aust-Agder, Norway) 39, 103
Sewerby (Yorkshire East Riding, England) 139
ship burial 19, 53, 117, 133, 134, 135, 136, 140-2, *49*
Sidonius, *Epistolae* 19
sīdsa 85
Sigrdrífumál 30, 98, 107, 115, 128
Sigurðarkviða inn skamma 103, 139
Skedemosse (Öland, Sweden) 26, 34, *34*
Skirnismál 33
Slusegård (Bornholm, Denmark) 140
Snape (Suffolk, England) 132, 136
Sneglu-Halla þáttr 79
Snorri Sturluson 25, 60, 62, 74, 79, 85, 93, 102, 103, 106, 107, 108, 109, 113, 136; see also *Edda*, *Gylfaginning*, *Heimskringla*, *Skaldsaparmál* and *Ynglinga saga* as well as individual named sagas.
Sögubrot 115, 116
Sörla þáttr 102, 110, 120
Sozomenos 51, 53
Spong Hill (Norfolk, England) 128, 130, 132, 138
St Peter's Broadstairs (Kent, England) 135
Staraya Ladoga (Volkhovsky, Russia) 93, *37*
stones, sacred 31, 44, 47,48, 49, 50, 60, 63, 66, 67, 114, 133, 134, 135, 142, *19*
Stora Ryttern (Västmanland, Sweden) 134
Strabo 109
Sturlu saga 84
Sturlunga saga 39

Sturm, see *Vita Sturmi*
Styrbjarnar þáttr Svíakappa 144
Summer king 116-7
Sutton Hoo (Suffolk, England) 17, 93, 134, 140, 141, *38*
Swallowcliffe Down (Wiltshire, England) 131

Tacitus, *Annales* 27, 66
Germania 16-7, 18, 19, 21, 30, 31, 44, 45, 50, 54, 61, 69, 71, 73, 76, 96, 100, 110, 112
Historiae 73, 78, 92
Taplow (Berkshire, England) 134
Theodore, Archbishop of Canterbury, *Penitential* 36, 39, 83, 87
Thietmar of Merseburg, *Chronicon* 15, 16, 74
Thor 19, 24, 29, 30, 34, 43, 46, 47, 48, 55, 59, 60, 61, 78, *23*, *24*, *25*
Thor's hammers 58, *28*, *29*
Thorsbjerg Mose (Schleswig, Germany) 26, 28, 68, 74, *34*
Þorsteins saga Víkingssonar 115
Þorvalds þáttr víðförla 48, 72
Tislund (Sjælland, Denmark) 47, 78
Tissø (Sjæland, Denmark) 66
Tollund Man from Bjældskovdal (Jylland, Denmark) 18, 23, *5*
Torsholma (Helgö, Uppland, Sweden) 46
Torslunda (Öland, Sweden) 93, *13*, (*37*)
Trajan's Column 120
Translatio S. Alexandri 50
trees 15, 17, 21, 24, 27, 31, 44-6, 47, 48, 67, 92, 95, 102, 114, 123, 143, *2*, *3*, *18*
Trelleborg (Sjælland, Denmark) 68
triclinium, 'dining room' 62, 64
Trögd (Uppland, Sweden) 78
'Troïlus and Zellandine' 103
Tuna (Uppland, Sweden) 140, 141
Tune (Østfold, Norway) 138
Turgeis 70, 72
Tynwald 77
Tysnes (Hordaland, Norway) 114

Ulfljótslög 47
Ulltuna (Uppland, Sweden) 134
Uppåkra (Skåne, Sweden) 65, 66, 93

Valsgärde (Uppland, Sweden) 140
Vanir 22, 54, 84, 85, 110, 113-7, 120, 121-4, 142; see also Frey, Freyja, Lytir, Nerthus, Njörd
Vápnfirðinga saga 70, 72
Västerby i Läby (Uppland, Sweden) 137
Vatnsdæla saga 33, 55, 86, 101, 119, 120
Vatzdæla saga 19, 21
vé, vé-bönd 68, 72, 77
Veleda 73, 92
Vellekla 68
Vendel (Uppland, Sweden) 140
Víga Glúms saga 29, 34, 84, 85
Vikar, sacrifice of 17, 23, 144
Víkarsbálkr 144
Vimose (Fyn, Denmark) 26, 68, 74, *34*
Vita Anskarii 30, 74, 146
Vita Bonifatii, see Willibald
Vita Eligii 34
Vita Guthlaci 136
Vita Karoli 117
Vita Lebuini 68, 76
Vita Liudgeri 28
Vita Sturmi 68
Vita Wilfridi 97
Vita Willibrordi, see Alcuin
Vix (Côte d'Or, France) 142
Völsunga saga 103, 112, 119, 120
Völundarkviða 31, 33, 115
Völuspá 32, 83-4, 85, 93, 101, 143, 144
völva, völur 86, 107, 111, 112
Vreta (Uppland, Sweden) 134

'Wanderer, The', Anglo-Saxon poem 32
weapons (axe, spear, sword) 17, 26, 27, 56, 58, 66, 87, 95, 96, 109, 118-9, 131, 137, 138, 139, 144; inverted 96, 109, 144, *39*, *43*, *50*
Weerdinge (Drenthe, Netherlands) 19
Weird Sisters 104
wells and springs 19, 31, 34, 44, 45, 46, 47, 67, 68, 79, 91, 93, 100, 102, 109, 123,
weoh 65
Widukind 50
Wilfrid, see *Vita Wilfridi*
Willibald, *Vita Bonifatii* 19, 23, 44, 46
Willibrord, see Alcuin
Windeby (Schleswig Holstein, Germany) 21, 22
Winter king, see 'Summer king'
Woden, Wotan, see Odin
Wulfstan, Archbishop of York, *Canons* 44, 91
Sermo Lupi ad Anglos 69, 70, 99
wyrd 104

xoanoi, see 'idols' and 'pillars'

Yde (Drenthe, Netherlands) 19, 23
Yeavering (Northumberland, England) 25, 50, 65, 135
Ynglinga saga 23, 55, 63, 70, 72, 73, 84, 87, 113, 115, 116, 117, 118, 119, 120, 121-3, 127, 135, 142, 144, 146
Ynglingatal 116